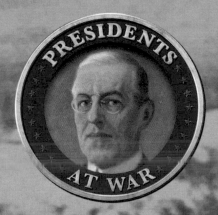

# HOW
# WOODROW
# WILSON
## FOUGHT
# WORLD WAR I

Samuel Willard Crompton

**Enslow Publishing**
101 W. 23rd Street
Suite 240
New York, NY 10011
USA

enslow.com

Published in 2018 by Enslow Publishing, LLC.
101 W. 23rd Street, Suite 240, New York, NY 10011

**Library of Congress Cataloging-in-Publication Data**

Names: Crompton, Samuel Willard, author.
  Title: How Woodrow Wilson fought World War I / Samuel Willard
    Crompton.
  Description: New York : Enslow Publishing, 2018. | Series: Presidents at war
    | Includes bibliographical references and index. | Audience: Grades 7–12.
  Identifiers: LCCN 2017004615 | ISBN 9780766085299 (library bound)
  Subjects: LCSH: Wilson, Woodrow, 1856–1924—Juvenile literature. |
    World War, 1914–1918—United States—Juvenile literature. | United
    States—Politics and government—1913–1921—Juvenile literature.
  Classification: LCC D766 .C76 2018 | DDC 940.3/73—dc23
  LC record available at https://lccn.loc.gov/2017004615
  Printed in the United States of America

336140804755105

**To Our Readers:** We have done our best to make sure all website addresses in
this book were active and appropriate when we went to press. However, the
author and the publisher have no control over and assume no liability for
the material available on those websites or on any websites they may link to. Any
comments or suggestions can be sent by e-mail to customerservice@enslow.com.

**Photo Credits:** Cover (Wilson), pp. 1, 5, 9, 19, 31, 42, 51, 64, 74, 84, 96, 106,
116 Library of Congress Prints and Photographs Division; cover, p. 1 (battle),
13, 17, 52, 72, 78, 101 Universal History Archive/Universal Images Group/
Getty Images; p. 6 Buyenlarge/Archive Photos/Getty Images; pp. 10, 23, 16, 25,
38, 40, 44, 50, 56, 68–69 Library of Congress Prints and Photographs Division;
p. 20 Education Images/Universal Images Group/Getty Images; p. 23 Library
of Congress/Corbis Historical/Getty Images; p. 29 WS Collection/Alamy
Stock Photo; p. 33 Time Life Pictures/The LIFE Picture Collection/Getty
Images; p. 34 Windmill Books/Universal Images Group/Getty Images; p. 48
Sheridan Libraries/Levy/Gado/Archive Photos/Getty Images; p. 58 Universal
Images Group/Getty Images; p. 60 Everett Historical/Shutterstock.com; p. 62
Niday Picture Library/Alamy Stock Photo; pp. 65, 82, 92, 99 Photo 12/
Universal Images Group/Getty Images; pp. 67, 94 PhotoQuest/Archive Photos/
Getty Images; p. 76 Keystone/Hulton Archive/Getty Images; p. 80 Pictorial
Press Ltd/Alamy Stock Photo; pp. 87, 90, 105, 107, 109, 112 Bettmann/Getty
Images; p. 97 Heritage Image Partnership Ltd/Alamy Stock Photo.

# CONTENTS

# INTRODUCTION

In the summer of 1914, America, and most of the rest of the world, was at peace. To be sure, there were tensions and flare-ups between various nations. But the overall theme was one of peace and the expectation that it would continue.

Forty-nine years had passed since the end of the Civil War, and in all that time Americans had not been called upon for any serious wartime sacrifices. The Spanish-American War, in 1898, had been a relative piece of cake, with the United States gaining large amounts of territory for rather little loss of life (more had died from disease than battle wounds). The various Indian Wars on the Great Plains had entailed no significant loss of life. Where foreign relations were concerned, a majority of Americans felt blessed.

Much, but not all, of this changed in the summer of 1914, when two great alliance systems went to war in Europe. The Allied Powers—consisting of Britain, France, Russia, Serbia, and a number of others—went to war against the Central Powers—consisting of Imperial

This map shows where the men of the American Expeditionary Force (AEF) landed in France, and the routes they took thereafter.

Germany, Austria-Hungary, Bulgaria, and the Ottoman Empire. Americans watched with horror, and some fascination, as the various Great Powers of Europe seemed determined to destroy each other.

Americans were glad to have a steady hand on the national tiller. Woodrow Wilson had only been in office a year and a half, but he demonstrated great calm as the Great War commenced. The son and grandson of Presbyterian ministers, Wilson believed that this—the second decade of the new century—represented a turning point in the affairs of humankind. Surely, he reasoned, the various peoples of Europe would come to their senses. Eventually they would recognize the benefits of peace, and he would be in a unique position. As the leader of the only nation which did not seek money, territory, or both, Wilson would act as the honest broker between the two sets of alliances, and bring the Great War to an end.

If anyone could have pulled this off, Woodrow Wilson was that man. The American president possessed great intellect, as well as an abiding faith that God was the author of history. Wilson had tremendous willpower, and his ability to move the average person with his speeches was unrivaled among the major leaders of the day.

But it was not to be. Too many powers had invested too much blood and treasure in the war. Therefore, with each passing month, the battlefield casualties increased, and the bitterness between the various nations rose. By 1916, the year Wilson was reelected to the presidency, millions of lives had been lost.

From his vantage point in Washington, DC, Wilson observed a terrible tragedy unfolding. Every man left dead on the battlefield increased the likelihood of future wars, which—thanks to technological advances—would be even more destructive. Therefore, in the late winter of 1917, the American president made up his mind. In order to help ensure future peace, he would propel his countrymen— white and black, immigrant and native born—into the most destructive war the world had ever seen.

# WILSON BEFORE
# THE CONGRESS

$A$ light drizzle of rain fell on Washington, DC, during the afternoon of April 2, 1917. Residents of the American capital city were not surprised or dismayed. The winter had been severe, and spring was later than usual. The really big news was not the weather, but the knowledge that President Woodrow Wilson would address both Houses of Congress at 7:30 p.m.

That the president would ask Congress for a declaration of war against Imperial Germany was understood by nearly everyone. America and Germany had drifted toward conflict for months, and it seemed natural—if regrettable—that the nations would soon go to war.

President Wilson and his entourage departed the White House at 6:15 p.m. Not only was the president surrounded by US Army personnel but there were also sharpshooters placed in buildings along his route. On this evening, no chances were taken with the president's security.

Arriving at the Capitol Building, President Wilson was brought inside and escorted to the chamber of the US House of Representatives. The chamber was the only room large enough to accommodate the members of the US House of Representatives and the US Senate, as well as the nine members of the US Supreme Court.

Entering the House chamber, President Wilson took heart from the outpouring of patriotic enthusiasm. Many senators and representatives waved American flags, and others shouted that they were willing to go to the battle-front themselves, if necessary. Removing his hat, President Wilson ascended the podium, adjusted his wire-rimmed spectacles, and began what he knew was the single most important speech of his career. "Gentlemen of the Congress,"[1] Wilson began.

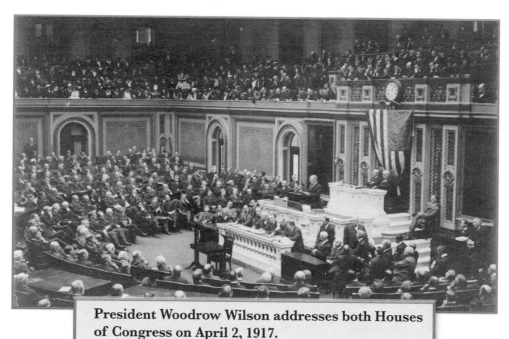

President Woodrow Wilson addresses both Houses of Congress on April 2, 1917.

# Names and Terms

One can refer to it simply as "Germany," but "Imperial Germany" is closer to the truth. Unlike the United States, Germany was not a democracy. It was ruled by Kaiser Wilhelm II and the leaders of his military establishment. In most of his letters and speeches, President Wilson intentionally employed the phrase "Imperial Germany" to discriminate between the German people and their government.

## The Crisis

Wilson had come before the joint Houses of Congress several times in the previous few years. Wilson enjoyed the art of speechmaking, and he had a high rate of success when it came to moving or persuading an audience. On the evening of April 2, 1917, however, the president had set himself a very high and significant test. He wanted to persuade the men and women (there was one female member of the US House at this time) to approve a declaration of war against Imperial Germany.

The crisis in German-American relations stemmed from the fact that Imperial Germany had conducted unrestricted submarine warfare in the North Atlantic. When World War I began three years earlier, Great Britain ruled the seas. Germany had introduced the submarine, however, and her U-Boats enjoyed considerable success, sinking the vessels of various nations. To address this problem was the major reason Wilson had come before the Congress.

"It is a war against all nations," President Wilson declared. "American ships have been sunk, American lives taken, in ways which it has stirred us very deeply to learn of."[2] America was not the only nation to suffer, however. Ever since Germany announced its practice of unrestricted submarine warfare, the ships of many nations had been attacked and sunk.

"There has been no discrimination," the president declared. "The challenge is to all mankind."[3]

For nearly three years, President Wilson had guided America in the path of neutrality. When World War I first began, he announced a neutral policy, and he even asked Americans to remain neutral in thought, as well as in action. Now, however, relations with Imperial Germany were strained to the brink.

"With a profound sense of the solemn and even tragical character of the step ... I advise that the Congress declare the recent course of the Imperial German Government to be in fact nothing less than war."[4] Wilson paused, and the members of the House and Senate rose to give a standing ovation. At that moment, the president knew his purpose was fulfilled, that the Congress would indeed vote the authorization. But he had another objective. He wanted to resolve this particular crisis, *and* he wanted to prevent future ones from even emerging.

## The Crusade

"We have no quarrel with the German people,"[5] Wilson declared. He went on to explain that it was the Imperial German government that had brought about the crisis. But now that America stood on the verge of war, Wilson wanted

This captured German mine layer shows the importance of the seas throughout all of the First World War. British and American fleets worked together to combat Germany at sea.

to insert something more profound and morally uplifting. He then uttered the eight words for which he would be forever famous.

"The world must be made safe for democracy."[6] This sentence, too, earned Wilson a standing ovation. He went on to say that America had no ulterior motives. She sought no land, no territory, and no conquest. Instead, she was about to enter the fray in order to ensure the survival of democracy, both at home and abroad.

The atmosphere in the House chamber was electric. The members of the Congress strained at the bit, eager to demonstrate their patriotism and loyalty. The president made them wait a little longer, however. Rather than come to a quick conclusion, he built to a steady and sure conclusion. Wilson was a practiced orator, one who knew how to "work" an audience. Never had he been better than on this evening.

"We can dedicate our lives and our fortunes,"[7] Wilson declared, adding that America and its people were privileged to risk everything in a sacred cause. America was ready to spend "her blood and her might for the principles that gave her birth."[8] He then concluded with the stirring words. "God helping her, she can do no other."[9]

## The Debate

After accepting the congratulations of many senators and representatives, Wilson went back to the White House. A close aide found him an hour later, in a very low spirit. When asked, Wilson replied that it was an awful thing to have to lead the nation into war. This aide—and many other people who knew the president well—marveled that Wilson could

## Religious Sentiments

Many American presidents—before and since—have evoked God and the protection of providence. Few of them, however, were as thoroughly qualified as Woodrow Wilson. He was the son and grandson and the nephew of Presbyterian ministers.

carry such contradictions. He could inspire the Congress, practically lift people out of their seats with his oratory. But he, himself, was feeling poorly about where the nation was headed.

The US Senate began its debate the following day. Though some senators expressed reservations, their voices were drowned out by those that asserted Imperial Germany had gone too far. America had to answer unprovoked aggression with war. The Senate voted 82–6 in favor of war.

The House of Representatives took a good deal longer than the Senate to reach a decision. Nearly two hundred members of the House rose to speak at various times during the long debate. Early in the morning of April 6, the House took up the vote. The final tally was 373–50 in favor.

Among the fifty House members who voted against war, one ballot was cast by Jeannette Rankin. A native of Montana, she had recently been elected and was the first female in American history to reach the halls of Congress. As the pressure built throughout the day on April 4,

Jeannette Rankin was the first woman to win election to the US House of Representatives.

Jeannette Rankin felt it. The *New York Times* described it this way:

"For a moment there was breathless silence. Then Miss Rankin rose. In a voice that broke a bit but could still be heard all over the still chamber she said: 'I want to stand by my country, but I cannot vote for war. I vote no.'"[10]

Despite the sentiments of Jeannette Rankin and forty-nine others, the war declaration passed the US House. As a result, the declaration was sent to President Wilson's desk.

Tradition has it that Wilson lingered a long time over the declaration; he was not pleased with the direction he, and the nation, had taken. But when he signed the document, Wilson did so with a flourish. The news went out by teletype and wire, and by the next morning, virtually everyone in America knew that the nation had gone to war.

This is a rare photo of President Wilson at a military camp. He was one of the most unmilitary of presidents, but circumstances forced him to become a wartime president.

# The Situation in April 1917

America and its elected representatives had made the critical decision, declaring war on Imperial Germany. Few people realized just how unprepared the nation was, however. There were roughly 130,000 men in the US Regular Army, and even fewer in the National Guard. The United States accepted Wilson's challenge, embarking on a great crusade for the sake of democracy everywhere. Many challenges would be faced and many sacrifices would be required in order for America to fulfill its pledge.

# CHAPTER TWO

# WILSON THE MAN, WILSON THE PRESIDENT

It has often been said that Woodrow Wilson was the most unlikely person ever to attain the White House. There is much truth to that notion.

Wilson was born on December 28, 1856, in Staunton, Virginia, a rural area that later played an important part in the American Civil War. Had he grown up in Staunton, Wilson would have seen much more of that conflict. Instead, his family moved to Georgia when Wilson was less than two years old.

Wilson grew up in Georgia and then South Carolina. In both states, his father was a prominent Presbyterian minister, as his father had been before him. Young Woodrow Wilson grew up with a profound sense of God's importance, and of the necessity of people carrying out God's will.

## Wilson's Youth and Education

For someone who would later stun the world with his intellect, Woodrow Wilson was a slow beginner. He did

This is Wilson's birthplace, in Staunton, Virginia. The family soon moved from there to Georgia.

not read well until the age of eleven. Biographers often comment on the influence exerted by his father, who was an all-powerful figure in the boy's life. These writers suggest that the young Wilson may have been overwhelmed by his father's example, that he suffered from an inferiority complex. Once Wilson got going, however, he did well.

After a short period at Davidson College, Wilson returned home. He then attended Princeton University, where he did well in his studies, and engaged in all sorts of extracurricular activities. He had a good singing voice, a pleasing manner, and his skill at writing became more pronounced. Even in these early years, there was an anxious quality to Wilson. He was eager to please, and was more occupied with religion than the average college student.

Of Wilson's religious faith there can be no doubt. From an early age, he read the Bible every day, and those who knew him best testified as to how he brought every decision—large or small—before God. The preacher's son had become an intellectual, but he stayed close to his father's enduring faith.

Wilson graduated from Princeton in 1879. His academic record was solid enough for him to gain acceptance into graduate school at the new Johns Hopkins University in Baltimore. There he studied political science, and it was as a graduate student that he became a true academic star. By now, Wilson was a presence on the university campus, well known to professors and fellow students. He had also found the great love of his life.

## Marriage and Family

Wilson first met Ellen Louise Axson during a visit to the town of Rome, Georgia. Like Wilson, she was the daughter of a Presbyterian minister. She was dreamy in an artistic

## Was Wilson a Genius?

Standard IQ measurements were not available when Wilson was a boy. Those who study his writings, however, are persuaded that Wilson had one of the highest IQs of all the presidents. He was the last president to write all of his own speeches, and the texts are today preserved in their original, something rare in our day and age.

sense, and she might have had a career as a watercolorist. Fate intervened, however. Wilson fell in love and proposed almost immediately.

Whether Ellen Axson immediately felt the same strong sentiment is not known. There is no doubt that they became one of the closest, and most passionate of couples, however. Following their marriage in 1883, they proceeded to have three children, all daughters. In his many letters written during their separations brought about by academic demands, Wilson makes plain their mutual passion. This was a couple that could not get enough of one other.

The three daughters were the apple of their father's eye. No matter how demanding his day—as a professor, a college president, and then a politician—Wilson found time to engage with his children. The family played board games, sang together, and were found—by virtually everyone who knew them—to be an exemplary family.

Wilson's domestic happiness was complete. He had great ambitions, however, and his struggle to be in the limelight never ceased, even when his heart was full.

## Professor

Wilson's first teaching job was at Bryn Mawr College, in Pennsylvania. He did not remain long and soon accepted another job, this time at Wesleyan University, in Middletown, Connecticut. Wesleyan was an all-female college, and Wilson was very much a ladies' man, meaning that he knew how to appeal to female sentiments. He therefore became a very popular professor, and when given the opportunity, he accepted a higher position, that of professor of political science at Princeton University. The move from Connecticut

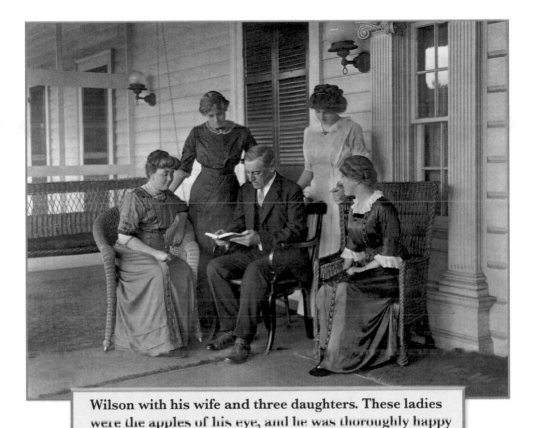

Wilson with his wife and three daughters. These ladies were the apples of his eye, and he was thoroughly happy in his domestic life.

to New Jersey was smooth, and Wilson soon became the professor most in demand on the Princeton campus.

Wilson was a truly gifted professor. Not only did he write out his lectures in longhand; he could throw them away if he desired and speak extemporaneously. Gifted in his choice of words, Wilson also had an excellent voice, which could soar or drop, according to his choice. Students flocked to his classes, and Wilson also found time to write several books. Of his many early writings, his *Constitutional Government in the United States* was the most pertinent to his long-range ambitions. In this book, Wilson freely confesses his admiration of the British constitution, and his doubts as to the success of the American Congress. By his thirties, he had become a strong advocate for presidential, as opposed to congressional, power and authority.

Wilson was now a genuine academic star. It was not that surprising that the Princeton University Trustees offered him the job of president of the university in 1902.

## University President

Wilson had a mixed record as president of Princeton. On one hand, he was a smash hit with local celebrities. One photograph from his Princeton days shows Wilson in full academic regalia, walking with none other than Andrew Carnegie, the richest man in America. Though he never showed much interest in money himself, Wilson was pleased to associate with men of great wealth. Sometimes it seemed as if he had become one of them, even though his pay as university president was only six thousand dollars.

At the same time, however, Wilson sometimes exhibited a strongly authoritarian bent. He expected, even demanded, complete loyalty from those who served in the university administration. It was during his years as Princeton president that Wilson came to believe in his own vision, to such an extent that he regarded any sort of disagreement as disloyalty. On most occasions, Wilson used his popularity with the trustees, and the student body, to overcome objections. He failed spectacularly on one occasion, however.

In 1907, Wilson embarked on a plan for academic reform. His proposals concerning classroom teaching were not radical. But his ideas about breaking up the eating clubs proved controversial. Princeton had many fraternities, and the members ate only with each other. Then too, the university was practically segregated between upperclassmen and freshmen, again with an emphasis on the dining clubs. Wilson attempted to break these up, to replace the separate dining facilities with a "quadrangle" plan he devised.

The plan was a dismal failure. Wilson encountered so much opposition that even the trustees refused to back him. What was most concerning, however, was the anger with which Wilson responded. As someone who frequently had his way, and was used to triumph, his failure to break down

**This photo shows Wilson with Princeton University students. He was in his natural element at the university.**

the separate dining establishments put him in a very sour mood. In private, he threatened to resign his position as president.

As things turned out, Wilson did not have to reject Princeton. Another opportunity came his way, and he soon shifted into the dynamic life of an American politician.

# Governor of New Jersey

Few American college professors—of Wilson's time or our own—succeed in politics. The two vocations call for rather different types of personality. Wilson was one of the rare exceptions, a talented college professor and administrator who could turn his attention to politics.

Thanks to his position as Princeton president, Wilson was acquainted with numerous men of wealth and power. In 1910, some of them approached him, asking if he was interested in running for governor of New Jersey. Privately, Wilson was delighted. Publicly, however, Wilson played coy. He said he would not seek the office, but that if the people asked, he would consider making the run.

Wilson's political savvy was unprecedented. Not only did the Democratic Party nominate him, but he ran a superb campaign. The college professor proved to be first-rate on the campaign trail. And in November 1910, he was elected governor of the Garden State.

Wilson proved a fine chief executive. A lifetime Democrat, he now identified with the Progressive wing of that party, meaning he intended to use the power of his office to make life better for the common person. In just a year, Wilson broke with the Democratic Party "machine" that brought him into office, and he initiated programs that broke the power of the railroad companies, which had long been the primary power in the state.

Wilson acted as if he were perfectly happy to be governor, that he had no higher ambitions. Outsiders saw the truth, however. The *New York Times* declared that the successful governor of New Jersey had presidential ambitions, and the *Times* proved correct.

In 1912, Wilson was presented with another opportunity.

# The 1912 Presidential Election

In 1912, the United States had been under Republican administration for eighteen years. Republicans had won the elections of 1896, 1900, 1904, and 1908. If all things were equal, the Republicans would be in line for a record fifth consecutive general election victory. The Republican Party split in two that year, however.

In 1912, the Republican Party nominated President William Howard Taft, the incumbent. But a section of the Republican Party broke away from the main part to nominate Theodore Roosevelt. He had served as president between 1901 and 1909. This break in the Republican party opened the way for Democratic success, and several important Democratic leaders turned to Woodrow Wilson.

Historians have often pointed out Wilson's lack of experience during the year of 1912. But it was that very lack of experience (and of political baggage) that made him appealing. Wilson had been extraordinarily popular as a Princeton professor, and he had been very effective as Princeton president. He had a high approval rate in the state of New Jersey. What Wilson did not have was a long political track record. That alone was enough to win the approval of many.

Wilson held himself aloof during the nomination process, but once endorsed by the Democratic Party, he campaigned heartily. The former professor once again turned out to be dynamic on the campaign trail. Wilson seemed to delight in the long train rides and the many speeches delivered from the back of the locomotive.

Election Day fell on Tuesday, November 5, 1912. Wilson won a four-way race by a plurality of the popular vote (Theodore Roosevelt came in second, followed by William Howard Taft, and Socialist candidate Eugene Debs came in last place). Wilson won handily in the Electoral College, however, and there was no doubt that he had scored a major political success.

## Wilson's Administration

From the day he first occupied the White House, in March 1913, Wilson proved an energetic president. He won the

## Was Wilson a Racist?

Sadly, the answer is yes. Wilson seldom spoke publicly on the matter, but his actions leave little doubt that he regarded whites as inherently superior to blacks. It can also be said, however, that Wilson was a racist who got better as he aged. During the First World War, he became more appreciative of African Americans, as he watched many of them give their all to the war effort.

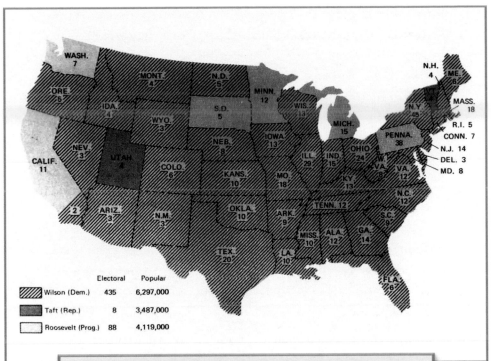

| | Electoral | Popular |
|---|---|---|
| Wilson (Dem.) | 435 | 6,297,000 |
| Taft (Rep.) | 8 | 3,487,000 |
| Roosevelt (Prog.) | 88 | 4,119,000 |

This Electoral College map of the 1912 presidential election shows that Wilson won in a landslide, beating both Republican Howard Taft and Bull Moose candidate Theodore Roosevelt.

affection, and admiration, of millions of Americans. Wilson delivered high-minded speeches to the Congress, but he also pushed legislation through Congress. The first federal income tax was instituted in 1913, and the Federal Reserve Board, intended to oversee the banking system, was established.

To be sure, Wilson's policies were not universally popular. He drew criticism, even anger, when he moved to segregate federal government employees. Having grown up in the Deep South, Wilson believed that separation of blacks and whites was a natural, even positive, thing. Wilson also proved unreceptive to visits from leading African Americans.

By the spring of 1914, Wilson had been in office for a year. He had already accomplished remarkable things, and some people spoke of him as one of the handful of "greats" to occupy the White House. The spring of 1914 should have been a very good time for Wilson. But, as is often the case in political life, tragedy came right alongside triumph.

Wilson's beloved wife, Ellen, became visibly ill in the late spring. By midsummer she was at death's door. And, at almost precisely the same time, Wilson faced the great international crisis of his time, the advent of the First World War.

CHAPTER THREE

# THE FIRST WORLD WAR BEGINS

On June 28, 1914, Franz Ferdinand, the archduke of Austria, paid a courtesy call to the city of Sarajevo in the province of Bosnia. The archduke and his wife, Sophie, were driven through the old, medieval city in a modern automobile. At around 2 p.m., a young Serbian nationalist stepped up to the running board and fired two pistol shots at point-blank range. Twenty minutes later, both the archduke and his wife were dead. This is how the *New York Times* reported the event.

"The assassin darted forth from his hiding place behind a house and actually got on the motorcar in which the Archduke and his wife were sitting. He took close aim first at the Archduke, and then at the Duchess. The fact that no one stopped him, and that he was allowed to perpetrate the dastardly act indicates that the conspiracy was carefully planned."[1]

The assassination of one couple does not seem sufficient to bring on a world war. In 1914, however, the

# Planned or Accidental

The assassination of Archduke Franz Ferdinand was certainly planned. The members of the Black Hand, the Serbian group, did not anticipate that it would result in a world war, however. Their intent was to foster a crisis within the Austro-Hungarian Empire, so that Bosnia would be able to separate itself. The assassination, therefore, was a planned event, while the world war that ensued was the result of a set of historical accidents.

various nations of Europe had a series of alliances of agreements—formal and informal—that made it quite possible for one event to bring on a great war. Russia, led by Czar Nicholas II, backed the little nation of Serbia. Austria-Hungary, led by aged Emperor Franz Josef, was determined to punish Serbia for the assassination of the archduke. To this point, it seemed as if the matter might remain an Eastern European conflict. Russia had an alliance with France, however. Fearing what Russia might do, Emperor Franz Josef appealed to Kaiser Wilhelm II, leader of Imperial Germany. And that was when things got much worse.

Despite all the claims made by his foes, Kaiser Wilhelm II was not a monster. Rather, he was a weak and neurotic man, who turned from one point of view to another with astonishing rapidity. Had he taken the time to consider the matter carefully, the kaiser might have held back. Instead, he gave what historians call the "blank check" to Austria, declaring that Germany would back its ally to the hilt.

One mistake and misunderstanding followed another. The basic sequence of events, however, is undeniable.

On July 28, 1914, one month after the assassination, Austria declared war on Serbia.

Two days later, Russia had mobilized many of her vast forces.

On August 1, 1914, Russia and Imperial Germany exchanged declarations of war.

And, most important of all, Imperial Germany invaded Belgium on August 3, 1914.

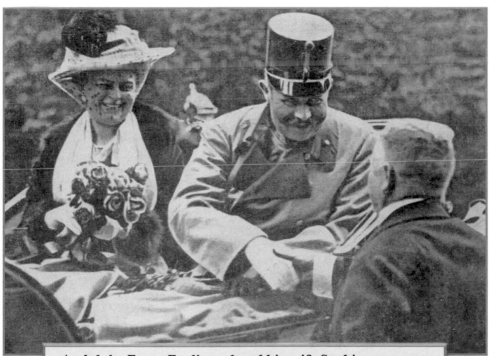

**Archduke Franz Ferdinand and his wife Sophie, moments before an assassin shot and killed them, in 1914.**

# Belgian Neutrality and Great Britain

That France would enter the war was a foregone conclusion, because of its alliance with Russia. Great Britain might have stayed out of the First World War, however. The change, which brought Britain into the war, was Imperial Germany's invasion of Belgium.

The neutrality of Belgium had been guaranteed by all the major powers in a series of treaties that dated back to the year 1839. Imperial Germany felt she had no choice, however. To invade northern France, her forces needed to

French troops in the trenches on the Western Front, perhaps from the year 1915. The war had not yet wrecked the morale of the various participants.

## Names of the Belligerents

The Allied Powers of Britain, France, Russia, Serbia, and others earned their name from the various alliances that brought them together. The Central Powers of Imperial Germany, Austria, Bulgaria, and the Ottoman Empire received their name from their geographic position. They occupied the central part of the map.

cross through Belgium. When Belgium refused to allow the Germans free passage, Germany invaded. Britain immediately declared war on Germany, setting up what was truly the First *World* War.

## American Neutrality

On August 4, 1914, Britain declared war on Germany, thereby turning the conflict into a world war. Britain, France, Germany, and Russia all possessed overseas' empires, and the peoples of those empires would be called upon to support the motherlands. The great question, in August 1914, however, was what America would do.

President Wilson was horrified by the events in Europe. More than most statesmen, he perceived the incredible tragedy that was about to unfold. At the same time, however, Wilson had a private tragedy. His beloved wife died on August 6, 1914, just two days after the war began in earnest.

Wilson was crushed. For twenty-eight years, Ellen Axson had been the steady foundation of his life. Her devotion enabled him to climb many mountains, in academics and then in politics. Wilson's grief was piercing, but he had to attend to the political crisis that stood right at his doorstep.

Ten days after his wife's death, Wilson issued a statement on the war.

"My fellow countrymen," the president's message began. "Every man who really loves America will act and speak in the true spirit of neutrality, which is the spirit of impartiality and friendliness to all concerned."[2] The words came as a surprise. Most people who knew the president were convinced—accurately—that he favored the Allied cause. Wilson had long admired the British constitution, and he surely hoped that England and her allies would prevail. But, reflecting on the fact that America had many immigrants, the president decided neutrality was the wisest policy. "The United States must be neutral in fact as well as in name during these days," the president declared. "We must be impartial in thought as well as in action."[3]

Some Americans criticized the president, declaring that the nation needed to join the Allied cause. A solid majority of Americans realized, however, that America would benefit from a neutral stance.

## The First Challenge to Neutrality

Americans were generally in favor of neutrality. This was because there were many Americans, from all walks of life, who were descended from English, Irish, or Scottish immigrants. At the same time, there were many, indeed millions, of Americans of German descent. To enter the war, on either side, would risk confrontations between the various ethnic groups of the United States.

During the winter of 1914–1915, the typical American felt blessed that war had not come. The European nations were at each other's throats, but the United States remained at peace. If the submarine had not arrived, America might have remained out of the war entirely. But, on May 7, 1915, a German U-Boat attacked and sank the *Lusitania*, the largest passenger ship of the day. Like her one-time sister ship, the *Titanic*, the *Lusitania* was an immense ocean liner that specialized in carrying well-to-do Americans to England.

Americans learned that the *Lusitania* had been torpedoed and sunk in the Irish Sea. Roughly 1,200 lives were lost, and 128 of those were American. Given that America was neutral, a majority of Americans were outraged. Many called for war against Germany.

President Wilson did not feel the same way. He, too, was distressed, even outraged. But in May 1915, the president saw the many benefits America had by remaining neutral. To enter the war, on the other hand, would expose the nation to all sorts of dangers. A few days after the *Lusitania* was sunk, Wilson gave a speech in Philadelphia. Addressing a group of people who had just gained full citizenship, the president declared that: "There is such a thing as a man too proud to fight."[4]

Wilson meant that America possessed the upper hand, in moral terms. As long as she stayed out of the war, she was the strongest force for good in the world. Wilson earned plenty of criticism at home for his decision to keep out of the war. He did send a stern diplomatic note to Germany,

RMS *Lusitania* was one of the finest, and most impressive, ships afloat, before she was torpedoed and sunk in 1915.

asserting America's rights as a neutral power. And for the moment, the German leaders backed down.

## Love and Wilson's Life

Wilson lost his beloved wife in August 1914. One year later, he met his second great love. Edith Bolling Galt was, like the president, a native of Virginia. She was a widow, and Wilson was charmed by her almost from their first meeting.

Wilson proposed marriage early in the relationship, but Galt was hesitant. She did not wish to appear too eager. Wilson's advisers, too, urged the president to wait. It was unseemly, they said, for him to move so quickly into marriage, when he had lost his wife only a year earlier. Wilson would not be thwarted, however. Throughout life, he had been heavily dependent on the women in his life.

His first wife and his three daughters had been essential to his well-being, but the daughters were now on the verge of adulthood. Wilson felt a strong need for female companionship.

Wilson continued to press the matter. In October 1915 he introduced his new love to the nation, at a World Series baseball game in Philadelphia. Two months later, Wilson and Galt were married in a small, private ceremony at her family's home.

Few Americans expressed criticism of the president at the time of his marriage. Americans seemed to understand that Wilson needed a helpmate, someone to stand with him in those difficult times. The president's aides reported they had not seen him so animated, or happy, in a long time.

## The Election of 1916

To Wilson, his marriage to Edith Bolling Galt was the most important event of the second half of his life. But to the

## Real or Pretended Neutrality?

When the *Lusitania* sailed from New York City, on May 1, 1915, she carried nearly one thousand passengers. At the same time, she carried, deep in her hold, a fair amount of explosives, which were to be sold to the Allied Powers. One can, in retrospect, say that America violated its own neutrality. There is no doubt that the United States profited, in material terms, from its neutrality in 1915 and 1916.

Edith Bolling Galt was a widow when she met the president. They married in December 1915.

Democratic Party, the great question was whether he would be reelected in 1916.

In 1916, the Republicans nominated Charles Evans Hughes, a former US Senator and a member of the Supreme Court. Hughes was only a bit to the right of Wilson in terms of domestic politics. The biggest difference between the two had to do with international relations. Hughes seemed more likely than Wilson to eventually intervene in the First World War. Knowing this, the Democratic Party used "He Kept Us Out of War" as their number-one campaign slogan.

Wilson campaigned energetically. He had always been happy when taking his case to the people, and he traveled, primarily by railroad, around the eastern states of the nation. Even so, Wilson knew that the western states would be crucial.

Election Day fell on Tuesday, November 7, 1916. On election night, it seemed that Charles Evans Hughes might win. Hughes led in many of the eastern states. When Wilson went to sleep that night, he was persuaded he had lost. But on waking the next morning, he learned that votes in the west were running in his favor. Wilson won California by fewer than ten thousand votes, but a win was a win. He won in both the popular vote and the Electoral College.

By almost any standard, Woodrow Wilson was an outstanding success. Not only had he managed to transition from academics to politics, but he proved himself a master of the latter. Not only had he been reelected, but he had, to this date, held to his campaign pledge. He had kept America out of the most destructive war the world had ever seen.

CHAPTER FOUR

# FROM NEUTRALITY TO BELLIGERENCE

In January 1917, Americans felt rather good about their situation. The economy was in good shape, thanks in part to the lucrative sales of war equipment to the Allied Powers. The country was at peace. America had taken none of the punishing losses that affected the peoples of Europe. What Americans did not realize was that the war, which had long been on their doorstep, was about to cross the threshold.

## Imperial Germany

The German high command was distressed by the long-lasting quality of the war. Nearly two million Germans had already lost their lives. In January 1917, the German high command resolved on an aggressive, even a desperate, policy. Germany would commence unrestricted submarine warfare. German U-Boats would attack the ships of any nation that sailed in the waters around the British Isles.

The German ambassador came to the office of the US Secretary of State on January 31, 1917. The ambassador delivered his unpleasant message, and then left. Just eight days later, President Wilson officially severed diplomatic relations with Germany.

# Czarist Russia

In March 1917, just weeks after Imperial Germany commenced unrestricted submarine warfare, the czar of Russia lost his throne. Czar Nicholas II was leader of the Romanov family, which had ruled Russia since 1613. The Russian war effort had been spectacular, with millions of men serving in the field, but it was also a terrible disaster. The Germans defeated Russia in most major battles, and they pressed deeper into Russian territory all the time.

The czar abdicated his throne on March 18, 1917. Days later, the czarist monarchy came to a complete end, and a provisional government was established. The new government quickly announced that it would stand by the treaties that were signed before the war began. Russia would remain one of the Allied Powers. The fact that the czar was gone made matters easier for President Wilson, however. If America entered the war, it would do so in the knowledge that Russia was on its way to becoming a democratic nation, not an absolutist one.

# The Zimmermann Telegram

At almost the same time that Germany upped the ante in submarine warfare, and when the czar fell from power, a German diplomat committed what can only be called a foolish error. Count Nicholas von Zimmermann sent a telegram to the German ambassador in Mexico. If war between

Czar Nicholas II looks very much in control, but he was forced to abdicate his throne in the winter of 1917.

America and Germany began, the ambassador should offer Mexico an alliance. And, assuming that all went well and their efforts were successful, Germany would eventually restore Texas, Arizona, and New Mexico to Mexico—the areas she had lost in the US–Mexican War of 1846–1848.

In retrospect, this was a terrible move. Mexico did not have much to offer Germany, in military terms, in 1917. Making everything worse, the Zimmermann Telegram was intercepted by British intelligence. The British diplomatic corps brought the telegram to the US State Department, and President Wilson learned that his potential foe had practically done all it could to bring him, and the United States, into the war.

# The Decision for War

President Wilson conferred with his Cabinet several times during February and March 1917. On almost every occasion, he found his Cabinet members more resolved than he was. Most members of the Cabinet believed the president now had no alternative but to declare war on Germany.

Members of the Cabinet could press and prod, but the decision was entirely up to the president. The precise moment at which Wilson made his decision is not known, but by the last week of March, he had set things in motion. Rear Admiral William Sims was sent to Great Britain, and Wilson spoke with enough senators and representatives to feel confident that the Congress would back his decision.

# The War Speech and the First Moves

As we saw in an earlier chapter, President Wilson went before the Joint Houses of Congress on the evening of

April 2, 1917. Four days later, he signed the official declaration of war on Imperial Germany.

America was now at war. The nation had enormous material and physical resources, and, given time, these would probably be sufficient for the Allies to win the war. But would American forces arrive in Europe in time? That was the biggest question of the moment.

## Wilson as War Leader

In the days and weeks that followed the declaration of war, President Wilson took firm control of the war effort. He confessed to members of his Cabinet that he was not schooled in the ways of war, but he reminded them that he was a quick learner. Everything in his background concurred with that statement.

Wilson's first, most pressing concern, was how to obtain the huge manpower required for the war. When war was

## Exhaustion of the Allies

In the winter of 1917, Britain, France, and Russia were almost equally exhausted. Russia had overthrown its czar and was attempting to become a democracy. Britain was suffering badly from the effects of German submarine warfare. And France, which had suffered more than one million dead, experienced the mutiny of numerous regiments on the Western Front.

## Over There

Tradition has it that George Cohan wrote "Over There" on the very day war was declared. Whether this is strictly true or not, "Over There" was an immediate hit, and it became America's war anthem. Even today, the words have the power to stir the listener.

declared, there were roughly 130,000 officers and men in the US Regular Army, placing it sixteenth in size among the major nations of the world. There were an additional one hundred thousand men in the National Guard(s) but Wilson was reluctant to commit the nation's only reserve to overseas combat.

In the first days, and perhaps the first three weeks of the war, President Wilson wanted to rely on volunteers for the augmentation of the Regular Army. The first results were disappointing, however. Less than one hundred thousand men enlisted in the first month. This was the case even though America had already found its war song.

As a result, Wilson and his Cabinet, announced that a military draft was necessary. It would be the first America had seen since the Civil War. Many Americans had heard of the Civil War draft and the riots that accompanied it. They were reluctant. But even as he pushed ahead for military conscription, the president also decided that wartime censorship would be necessary. Naturally, the president did

This poster advertises the famous song "Over There" which became the image for American patriotism during the First World War.

not label it censorship. Rather, the Committee on Public Information (also known as the CPI) was established.

Though the president, the secretary of the army, and the secretary of the navy were all members of the CPI, the meetings themselves tended to be run by George Creel. A brilliant newspaperman, Creel was recruited because of his skill in writing advertisements. Before long, many people called it the "Creel Committee."

# Civilian Leadership of the Armed Forces

Though generals and admirals would conduct the war on the ground and on the water, civilian leaders directed everything from Washington, DC. In 1917, the secretary of the army was Newton Baker, and Josephus Daniels was secretary of the navy.

Born in West Virginia in 1871, Newton Baker was the son of a Confederate soldier. Baker first met Woodrow Wilson at Johns Hopkins University, in 1892, and in 1916, the president appointed Baker the new secretary of war. The odd thing was that Baker was a committed pacifist, a person who did not believe in the virtues, or efficacy, of war.

Remarkably, Baker overcame his scruples and served as an effective and competent secretary of the US Army. He did not consider himself a military expert, and was content to leave much responsibility to the generals on the ground. At the same time, however, Baker oversaw the effort from Washington, DC.

Born in Washington, North Carolina in 1862, Josephus Daniels was orphaned before he reached the age of three. The Daniels family had moved from Washington

Newton D. Baker was Secretary of the US Army during the First World War. Well-liked, he set a record for conscientious service.

to Wilson, North Carolina, and Daniels's father, who was notorious as a Union man living in the South, was shot and killed by a sharpshooter. Not surprisingly, Daniels grew up to become an ardent pacifist. Daniels became a successful newspaperman before he entered Wilson's Cabinet as secretary of the US Navy in 1913.

Once the war began, despite Daniels's dislike for violence, he served as an effective secretary of the navy. Daniels relied on the actions of his number-one subordinate, the young Franklin D. Roosevelt, to a large degree. Like his distant cousin Theodore Roosevelt, Franklin Roosevelt rose through New York state politics before entering the Wilson administration.

Wilson was about as unlikely a wartime president as the nation could have. Even though he grew up in rural circumstances, hunting had never had any appeal for him and he was not much for guns. Wilson did have great intellect and powers of concentration, however, and he brought these to bear on the war effort. One of the most important meetings Wilson had was with the man Secretary Baker had chosen as commanding general in the field.

CHAPTER

FIVE

# ADMIRALS AND GENERALS

Even before he went to Congress asking for the declaration of war, President Wilson dispatched Rear Admiral William Sims to London. Born in Ontario, Canada, in 1858, Sims was the son of American parents. He graduated from the US Naval Academy at Annapolis in 1880, and commenced a distinguished career. Sims was not a superstar, either at the Academy or in the US Navy. He was the type of officer who rose steadily and slowly through the ranks.

In late March 1917, Sims was sent to London to act as the highest-ranking US Navy leader. He arrived in London just two days after war was declared, and he was immediately thrown into the whirlwind. Admiral Sims soon met Admiral Sir John Jellicoe, leading officer of the British Royal Navy. What Jellicoe told Sims was shocking.

If Britain did not find an answer to the problem caused by German U-Boats, she would be forced from the war in a matter of months.

Admiral William Sims was a quiet diplomat, guiding cooperation between the British and American navies through World War I.

# Sims and the British Admiralty

At first, Admiral Sims found it difficult to believe Admiral Jellicoe. How could Britain, which possessed the world's greatest surface navy, be endangered by the German U Boats? In a rather short time, Sims learned the reason. Britain's navy was unchallenged on the surface of the seas, but the German submarines had already sunk six hundred thousand tons of British merchant shipping. If this continued through the summer of 1917, Britain would be forced to break with her allies, and seek a separate peace.

As powerful as Great Britain was, she was vulnerable to any disruption in the flow of trade and supplies from aboard. This was especially true where corn and wheat were concerned: she relied on large amounts of these from Canada and Australia. Admiral Sims began to see the situation as just as desperate as the British leaders portrayed it. Something had to be done.

One of Sims's first proposals was that America and Britain work together to establish a convoy system, under which merchant ships of both nations would be protected by warships and destroyers (lighter vessels which could pursue submarines). Sims's idea was shot down by the British Admiralty, which claimed that this method had already been attempted. Sims refused to quit, however. He made the proposal again and again, and in the early summer of 1917, British and American ships began to cooperate in convoys.

The results were nothing short of remarkable. The Germans submarine effort peaked around the first of July 1917, and half a million tons of Allied shipping were sunk that month. But almost immediately afterward, from the first of August, German submarine success began to wane. There were two reasons. First, the Americans and British worked well together. Second, American ingenuity brought a handful of new weapons to the battle scene. The British had already experimented with depth charges, aimed at German submarines. A brand-new American intervention allowed the charges to be dropped more methodically and with better results.

Then too, Admiral Sims persuaded the British to attempt another approach. Beginning in the winter of 1917–1918, British and American ships dropped a vast quantity of unexploded mines in the North Sea and the English Channel. Perhaps a dozen German submarines were caught in the net and destroyed, and that loss alone helps to account for a flagging in the German war effort.

In one other way, Admiral Sims was instrumental to the Allied war effort. Right from his first day in London, Sims took a second-class position, meaning that he did not contest with the British admirals. Other American naval commanders followed Sims's lead. While the Americans sometimes resented what they considered British high-handedness, everyone knew of Britain's great naval tradition. It was better, and more effective, to allow the British to hold the bragging rights.

Admiral Sims was extraordinarily effective, at least in part because he did not seek credit for his actions. The British-American efforts bore fruit, especially when American soldiers were sent to France. The convoy system kept the great majority of them safe.

# General Pershing

In April 1917, President Wilson asked secretary of the army, Newton Baker, to select an outstanding person to lead what became the American Expeditionary Force (often referred to as the AEF). As mentioned in the previous chapter, Secretary Baker did not possess military experience. He was a fine judge of character, however, and this was exemplified when he chose Major-General John Joseph Pershing.

Born in Laclede, Missouri, in 1860, Pershing had something in common with President Wilson. Both men grew up with the American Civil War as their most lasting memory. Laclede was a Union town that was invaded by Confederate cavalry, and young Pershing never forgot witnessing the events.

Pershing went to the US Military Academy at West Point, but his ambition—at that time—was either for the law, or for a career in teaching. Four years at West Point showed Pershing's quality as a leader of men, however. Six feet tall and ramrod straight, Pershing simply looked like a soldier, the very best kind. After graduation, Pershing served as a captain of cavalry in the American West. Because he frequently commanded African American soldiers, Perishing was called "Black Jack," a nickname that suggested more scorn than admiration. Pershing went on to serve with distinction in the Spanish–American War, where his commanding officer referred to him as "the coolest man under fire I ever saw."[1] Pershing then served in the Philippines, and by the time World War I began, he was a major general, and among the five or six most admired officers in the US Regular Army.

John J. Pershing was one of the toughest and most self-reliant of all World War I commanders.

Secretary Baker selected Pershing for his leadership qualities. Though he was fifty-seven, Pershing looked as active and fit as ever. Secretary Baker brought Pershing to the White House on May 21, 1917, for his one and only meeting with President Wilson. The president declined to talk about specific policies or campaigns. Instead, he simply pledged that Pershing would have a free hand, and that he would back him all the way. The trust Wilson showed endeared him to General Pershing, and helped to bring out his finest qualities. Days later, Pershing and his staff of about 180 men sailed from New York City.

# Meeting the British

A week later, Pershing and his staff landed in Liverpool, on England's west coast. The Americans were met by a parade, complete with marching band. The first English men and women to see the Americans were impressed by Pershing his physical fitness and serious demeanor worked in his favor yet again. Hours later, Pershing and his staff went aboard the royal train, and were taken quickly to London.

In a remarkably short time, General Pershing was introduced to General Sir Douglas Haig, the number-one British commander in the field, and to King George V. Both men liked the American, whom they found serious and well intentioned. The general and the monarch were both surprised by Pershing's most significant answers, however. General Haig and King George V mistakenly believed that the United States could send half a million men in a hurry, and both men declared that this was vitally important. Pershing did not shrug. Neither did he attempt to disguise the plain facts. America had very few men who

King George V was a fine war leader for the British, and a good friend to the Americans he encountered.

were trained and at the ready. She could only commit a small number in 1917. More would follow in 1918, he said.

To the British, this was bad news. They had been spoiled by Admiral Sims, who accommodated their wishes and desires. General Pershing, on the other hand, made it plain that he would lead an *American* army, and not groups of men to be broken up and used as replacements. No amount of diplomatic finesse could change Pershing's mind on this point. Days later, Pershing and his staff embarked for France.

# Paris and Lafayette

Landing at the old port of Boulogne, Pershing and his officers came ashore to see a French parade. Hours later, they were on a special train headed for Paris. On arriving in the French capital, Pershing found himself bombarded by requests, even demands. Much like the British, the French believed America ready to dispatch hundreds of thousands of men. This was far from the case.

Pershing used his limited French to ingratiate himself. He moved his headquarters to a mansion in Paris, one owned by a wealthy American. Right from the beginning, Pershing felt a great deal of pressure exerted by French officers and politicians. Perhaps the most insistent were General "Papa" Joffre, hero of the Battle of the Marne in 1914, and General Henri Pétain, hero of the Battle of Verdun in 1916. Both leaders insisted that France needed "men, men, men."[2]

Only as he came to know these men better did Pershing learn of the series of mutinies that crippled the French armies in the winter of 1917. Regiments, even divisions of

Henri Pétain, French general, receives the baton of a Marshal of France, in 1918.

# Trench Warfare

World War I was characterized by rapid movement and maneuvers in the summer and early autumn of 1914. Once the first big battles were fought, however, both sides settled into the tedium, and exhaustion, of trench warfare. Allied soldiers dug enormous trenches, sometimes thirty feet deep, and their Central Powers opponents did the same. In between the two sets of trenches was the area called no-man's-land, and with good reason. Anyone who ventured into that area was soon the recipient of machine-gun fire, as well as exploding hand grenades.

French troops simply refused to fight in any more offensive actions. They had had their fill of trench warfare.

Pershing told the French the same as he had told the British: the United States had plenty of men, but they first had to be trained and equipped. No great infusion of manpower was possible in 1917, he declared.

Pershing realized, however, that French morale was very low. He had to do something to stiffen the resolve of the Allies. Pershing, therefore, agreed that a group of Americans, the first battlefield troops to arrive, would parade through Paris on the Fourth of July 1917. Privately, Pershing was worried. He feared his men might not make a significant impact. Perhaps the Parisians would look down their noses at this, the first group of "sturdy rookies," as Pershing described them.

Pershing need not have worried. Though the Americans that paraded through Paris on July 4, 1917 were rookies, they were hale and healthy, and the Parisians looked on them with admiration, and perhaps some envy. The typical Allied soldier was underfed compared to these Americans, and that is where the expression "Doughboy" originated. The Americans were so well fed that they looked like doughboys to the French observers.

After parading down the Champs Élysées, in the very heart of the city, Pershing and his men marched to the Picpus Cemetery, where the Marquis de Lafayette was buried. Virtually all Americans knew of the marquis, who crossed the Atlantic to help them during the American Revolutionary War (dozens of towns and counties in the United States were named for him). To honor Lafayette in

General Pershing speaks to French and Americans at the tomb of Lafayette in Paris.

this moment was the finest diplomatic move Pershing could make.

After laying a wreath on Lafayette's tomb, General Pershing gestured to Captain Charles E. Stanton, asking him to say a few words. Pershing knew that he was not a great speaker; he hoped that Stanton could do better. And Captain Stanton outdid himself. Though he said fewer than one hundred words, they went straight to the point, the essence of the matter. And Stanton concluded with the memorable, and stirring words, "Lafayette, we are here!"[3]

CHAPTER SIX

# THE WAR AT HOME

From his vantage point in Washington, DC, President Wilson could not see the war very clearly. This was not due to any fault of his own. Rather, it was a necessary consequence of the fact that World War I was fought three thousand miles from home.

Knowing that he could make mistakes by attempting to micromanage the war effort, Wilson saved most of his energy for the (figurative) battles at home. He trusted General Pershing, Admiral Sims, and others to wage war while Wilson provided the means.

Wilson knew that his British and French allies needed men and more men, above all else. Wilson was determined that the men he would send would be well prepared, however. And to the Presbyterian minister's son, this meant far more than uniforms, shoes, and rifles. The Americans Wilson sent needed to be men of high moral caliber.

This was never more apparent than when Wilson issued a statement about the Bible.

Newly printed Bibles were packaged and then shipped to US soldiers in the field.

# The Bible

In August 1917, Wilson had a statement circulated to all US soldiers, sailors, and marines. He began with these words:

"The Bible is the word of life. I beg that you will read it and find this out for yourselves—read, not little snatches here and there, but long passages that will really be the road to the heart of it."[1] These were not throwaway words. Wilson seldom, if ever, let a day pass without reading Scripture. But in his direct approach to the US personnel, Wilson went further than any previous chief executive. Not even George Washington in the American Revolution or Abraham Lincoln, in the Civil War, made such frequent references to the Bible and the Almighty.

In his statement, Wilson went on to say that the Bible presents the only clear guide for men who wish to be truly happy: "loyalty, right dealings, speaking the truth, readiness to give everything for what they think their duty."[2]

## The Selective Service

In May 1918, the Wilson administration announced that military conscription—or the draft—would begin in June. America had not seen a military draft since the Civil War. Though rather few people were old enough to remember, the 1863 draft had been deeply controversial. Terrible riots had ensued, with the worst ones in Manhattan in July 1863. Many people feared something similar would happen in 1917.

But when draft day came, in June 1917, the critics were astounded. The Wilson administration did something very intelligent in leaving control of the draft boards to men (and sometimes women) in the local communities. Though the draft numbers were drawn in Washington, DC, with a blindfolded Secretary Baker making the first pick, it was local people who registered the young men, those between the ages of twenty and forty.

Virtually no major protests marred the registration process. Americans, young and old, male and female, seemed resigned to the process. And, in a remarkably short time, more than one million men were summoned for duty. Though the Wilson administration was sometimes heavy-handed, as will be seen below, Secretary Baker and his officials pulled off a major coup where the draft was concerned.

A blindfolded Newton Baker—the Secretary of War—draws the first lottery numbers for the Selective Service, in 1917.

# Hard Line on Dissent

At the same time that he urged the soldiers and sailors to read the Bible, Wilson undertook a series of steps to quash dissent. Though two-thirds of the American public backed the war effort, that left another third that was either ambivalent or downright opposed. The Committee on Public Information (often called the Creel Committee) censored the newspapers and even took leading journalists to court.

Quite a few prominent Americans were opposed to the war. Helen Keller, one of the most beloved of all Americans, won enmity from many for her speeches against the war. John Reed, an outstanding journalist, declared that the war was a fiction, dreamed up by Wall Street bankers and arms merchants. And there was no arguing with the fact that American industry benefited from the massive production of war materiel.

The Creel Committee had an answer. Roughly 75,000 men and women were hired by the committee to give short speeches in favor of the war. Though urban centers such as Philadelphia and Baltimore saw the largest number of these "Five Minute Men," plenty of rural communities also received speakers. The speakers linked the American struggle of 1917 with that of 1776. America had to fight for its place in the world, they said, and Americans also had to fight for the cause of democracy around the globe.

The Five Minute Men were very successful. By the end of 1917, it seemed as if 90 percent of Americans were solidly behind the war effort. This figure might not have been a solid one, but there is little doubt that the Wilson administration had Americans "in line" by the end of 1917.

## Taking the Railroads

Toward the end of 1917, it became apparent that the military draft and the eventual shipment of men overseas

was succeeding. Wilson and his administration realized that American shipping could not handle all the work of transporting the men to France—that British ships would be needed. But the single most pressing issue had to do with overland transportation.

The American railroad system was roughly fifty years old. It had been built by a handful of wealthy families, all of which had—quite naturally—concentrated on increasing their wealth. The railroad system ran rather well in peace-time, but it was thoroughly inadequate to meet the wartime effort. Millions of tons of materiel, both for the war and for civilian population needs, had to be transported. Virtually everyone in the Wilson administration concurred that the railroad system needed to be changed.

Therefore, just as Christmas approached, the president seized control of the railroads. He did not ask the permission of Congress. He did not consult with leaders of the opposition party. Wilson simply declared, in an executive order, that the federal government had taken control of the railroad system.

This photo of a US Army cantonment, in Iowa, shows the incredible strength and muscle of the American forces. Only the United States could produce more bread than its soldiers could eat.

Americans did not react. They were already used to the government asking more of them. Now the government was demanding sacrifice by some of the large corporations.

# The Fourteen Points

As 1917 turned to 1918, Wilson had much to feel good about. America had more than two million men either under arms or in training, and the first significant numbers had just begun crossing the Atlantic. The United States had placed itself on a wartime footing. Though great work, and sacrifices, still lay ahead, the president felt emboldened to make a strong statement about American war aims. On January 8, 1918, Wilson went to the Capitol building to address both Houses of Congress. His address has ever since been known as the "Fourteen Points" speech.

Wilson began the speech by noting that the Central Powers showed signs of willingness to make peace. He therefore laid out what he believed was the American approach to peace, and what he thought was necessary to make this—the Great War—the last of all great military conflicts.

First and most important was the end to secret diplomacy and negotiations. Wilson declared that "open covenants of peace, openly arrived at,"[3] were essential to making, and preserving, world peace. His second point had to do with "absolute freedom of navigation upon the seas."[4] Wilson knew his British ally would not take kindly to this point, but he believed it essential. The third of Wilson's fourteen points had to do with removing economic barriers to trade. The fourth of his points addressed the issue of armaments, and he called for measures to ensure that "national armaments will be reduced to the lowest point consistent with domestic safety."[5]

The fifth of the Fourteen Points was, in some ways, the most controversial. Wilson called for a "free, open minded, and absolutely impartial adjustment of all colonial claims."[6] This was bad news for Britain and France, but also for Italy and Germany. Most of the nations that entered the Great War in the summer of 1914 possessed colonial empires. Wilson now opened the door to an adjustment, which might well result in the end of those empires.

The sixth of the Fourteen Points called for the evacuation of all Russian territory. The seventh called for the restoration of Belgium, and the absolute guarantee of her future neutrality. The eighth of the Fourteen Points called for the restoration to France of the provinces of Alsace and Lorraine, which had been taken by Imperial Germany at the end of the Franco-Prussian War, in 1871. The ninth of the Points called for an adjustment of the frontiers and boundaries of Italy, and the tenth point called for the peoples of Austria-Hungary to be accorded national autonomy. Romania, Serbia, and Montenegro should be evacuated — this was the eleventh of the Fourteen Points. The Ottoman Empire should be reduced to the lands that were properly part of Turkey, and the Straits of the Dardanelles should be internationalized. The thirteenth Point addressed the issue of Poland, which was of no small interest to America, which had millions of Poles. President Wilson called for a brand-new "independent Polish state."[7] Wilson saved his single most important point for last, however. He called for a "general association of nations"[8] to gather and be made permanent. Only by forming such a group

Poland had been divided between its neighbors in the late 18th century. But the new Polish republic was proclaimed in 1918.

this way could the peace and security of all nations—large and small—be guaranteed. He felt that if all the nations were devoted to solving future problems through discussion and diplomacy, the world would become a safer and more secure place.

The senators and representatives listening to Wilson's words applauded politely. Some of them were, quietly, weary of President Wilson's high-minded approach to international politics. But the American people liked the Fourteen Points rather well. If millions of young Americans were to fight and perhaps die overseas, there should be a strong commitment to American principles. And the Four-teen Points were received with unfeigned joy by millions of people in other nations.

Woodrow Wilson—and the nation he led—had come a long way in ten months. In April 1917, America declared war on Germany, and acted its part as one of the leading belligerents. In January 1918, America seemed ready to take on a new mantle, one of protecting peace and liberty for millions of people around the globe.

Before world peace could be achieved, America still had to prove her worth on the battlefield, however.

# THE CRISIS

One can argue that the entire four years between August 1914 and November 1918 represent one long crisis for the world. But it can also be argued that the late winter and early spring of 1918 represented the keenest and sharpest point of that long crisis. It was during March, April, and May 1918 that Imperial Germany and her allies came closest to winning the First World War.

## The Treaty of Brest-Litovsk

Early in March 1918, Imperial Germany and the new Bolshevik government in Russia signed the Treaty of Brest-Litovsk. Russia's new leaders, who would soon be called Communists, signed away one fifth of Russia's European land space in exchange for peace. The treaty was punitive in the extreme, indicating what might happen to the other Allied nations, if Germany won the war.

Russia's new leaders had little choice. Imperial Germany had proved itself dramatically superior on the

# Lenin and Trotsky

In the spring of 1917, as Russia's provisional government got off the ground, Vladimir Ilyich Ulyanov (better known simply as "Lenin") and Trotsky took charge of the Bolshevik movement in Moscow and St. Petersburg. Both were men of courage and great intelligence. By November 1918, they had overthrown the Provisional Government, and by March 1918, they stood atop Russia. They knew each other, and their followers, as Bolsheviks, but over time the world came to know them as Russia's Communist leaders.

battlefield. If Russia did not sign the treaty, things might become much worse. Russia, therefore, exited the war. This led to new policies and programs in Imperial Germany.

# Von Ludendorff and Von Hindenburg

By March 1918, Kaiser Wilhelm II was a helpless wreck. Four years of war had played havoc with his nerves. The kaiser, therefore, quietly stood aside while two military men assumed nearly dictatorial powers.

Born in Posen, Prussia, (today it is part of Poland) in 1847, Paul von Hindenburg was the epitome of a German field marshal. Of aristocratic blood, he had spent his life in the service of the German military. Von Hindenburg

**Lenin and Trotsky were the formidable one-two punch that led to the success of the Bolshevik Revolution in the autumn of 1917.**

was old enough that he could recall the triumphs of the Franco-Prussian War (1870–1871), and he yearned to lead Germany to victory in 1918.

Born near Posen, in 1865, Erich von Ludendorff came from a comfortable middle-class background. Like von Hindenburg, von Ludendorff had given his life to the German military. Unlike von Hindenburg, von Ludendorff did not have an aristocratic pedigree. Yet of the two, Ludendorff became the more important.

Between them, these two highly skilled men planned to win the war. It was essential, they agreed, to strike hard and fast before the Americans arrived in great numbers.

## Transfer to the West

The moment the Treaty of Brest-Litovsk was signed, entire divisions of the German army began transferring from the Eastern to the Western Front. The German railroads made this possible. By the third week of March, perhaps a million German soldiers were on the move, and nearly all of them were headed toward the giant showdown against Britain and France.

On March 21, 1918, the British and French defenders on the Western Front, were shaken by an immense German artillery bombardment. Hundreds of thousands of shells were hurled at the Allied lines, and twenty-four hours later the Germans attacked in full force.

Historians call these General von Ludendorff's "sledge-hammer blows." Four years of trench warfare persuaded the German high command that they must win in the spring of 1918 or be doomed to defeat. The Germans, therefore, attacked in a new style, one that allowed small groups of their men to pass through the Allied lines, and then to set up positions in their rear.

The early German attacks succeeded. Perhaps it was the rundown quality of the British and French defenders who were exhausted. Then again, it may have been the sheer desperation of the German assailants, who knew it was then or never. In either case, the Germans penetrated

Hindenburg and Ludendorff were the masterminds of Germany's war effort.

the Allied lines, and made significant gains. In some areas they moved thirty miles in a week. This sounds small in present-day terms, but no place on the Western Front had seen that much territory change hands in four years of war.

# The Resistance

The Allies were in rough shape. The French were able to maintain only defensive operations, and even these were limited. The British fought stoutly, but were in danger of being overwhelmed. And the Americans only had three hundred thousand men in the field.

# Pershing's Vow

In the eight months since he first arrived in France, General John Pershing had accomplished wonders. He seemed to be everywhere, shoring up old units, and instructing new ones. Pershing did not, on the whole, win the love of his soldiers. He was too spit-and-polish, too old-fashioned West Point for that. But if he never gained the favor of the enlisted man, Pershing soon became the darling of the American officer corps. He was fierce at times, and demanded great dedication to the job at hand. At the same time, he was fair, and utterly loyal to subordinates who gave their all.

In the spring of 1918, Pershing came under pressure—time and again—to throw the first American ground troops in as replacements for worn-out British and French regiments. On each occasion Pershing refused. President Wilson had granted Pershing great latitude on most military matters. On one point, however, the president had been adamant. The Americans that went to France must act together, as an American army.

## The Rookies

By May 1918, at great cost to themselves, the German forces created large bulges in the Allied lines. This was the first time since the late summer of 1914 when it was possible to envision a major collapse on the Western Front. Encouraged by their success, the Germans threw even more men into the fray, and by late May, the French were in full retreat.

The way to Paris lay open. Making matter worse, the Germans deployed an enormous new siege cannon, large enough that it could hurl projectiles a distance of sixty, even

This, the most famous photograph from the entire war, shows Americans fighting at Belleau Wood, in June 1918.

seventy miles. Parisian civilians came under long-distance fire for the first time in the war.

No one knew better than General Pershing how severe the crisis was. If the Germans broke completely through the French lines, his Americans would be left with nothing but the coast to defend. Pershing, therefore, exerted every effort, and the first large-scale American forces began to arrive in the last days of May. This was not a moment, or an hour, too soon.

On the first of June 1918, victorious German forces entered Belleau Wood, an area forty miles northeast of Paris. They had already crossed the Marne River, and Paris looked well within their grasp. This was when the Germans had their first encounter with US forces.

Perhaps ten thousand Americans were on hand as the Battle of Belleau Wood raged. The majority of Americans in the fight were US Marines, and they showed the dogged determination for which their corps was famous. Germans reported to their commanding officers that the new foe was more stubborn than any they encountered previously. Day after day, the Battle for Belleau Wood raged, and by June 22, 1918, it was evident the Americans had won. At great cost to themselves, Pershing's sturdy rookies turned the tide. Paris would not fall.

The most dangerous point had passed. And the Americans—raw though they were—played a huge role in stemming the tide.

# Pershing and Foch

During the most severe point of the military crisis, the British, French, and Americans agreed to make Marshall

**General Pershing meets with Field Marshal Ferdinand Foch.**

Ferdinand Foch the supreme Allied war leader in the field. An artilleryman, whose experience stretched back to the 1890s, Foch was not the ideal choice. His views on technology had been established long ago, and he was not very receptive to new ones. As a fighting general, however, Foch was superb.

Foch was determined to take the battle to the Germans, who had inflicted so much damage, both to the French army and to French civilians. Foch saw the value of the fresh, new American units, arriving in larger numbers each day, and he wanted to use them in a piecemeal fashion. One of the most famous—and reported-on—episodes of the war took place when Foch drove to Pershing's headquarters, to demand that the Americans be broken up among his own men.

As had happened so many times, the French general demanded that the Americans be broken up. When Pershing refused, Marshal Foch asked, his voice dripping with sarcasm, whether Pershing and his men really wanted to be in the fight.

"Most assuredly, but as an American army and in other ways," was Pershing's reply.

CHAPTER

EIGHT

# THE FINAL PUSH

The First World War contains many ironies. One of the most poignant is that the last nation to enter was the one that did the most to win the conflict. Britain, France, Serbia, and a host of other allied nations had been in the war for three long years before the first American appeared on the battlefield. Even so, there is little doubt that the United States delivered the final, and most punishing set of blows.

This, naturally, leads to the question: would the Allied Powers have won without America? The chances are that the war would not have been won by either side, and that the two exhausted sides would have come to some sort of agreement. And using this logic, or frame of argument, it seems likely that the end results of the First World War would have been even worse than was the case.

## The Allies in July

In July 1918, it was almost certain that Imperial Germany could not win the war. The vast German forces still looked impressive, but many of the men had been fighting for four long years. They could not keep up the effort for long.

Much the same can be said for the British and the French. Both peoples took heart by the way von Ludendorff's sledgehammer blows failed—in May and June of 1918—but neither nation was ready for a massive new effort. The only nation which could put fresh troops on the ground was the United States, and those Americans came in the nick of time.

Toward the end of July 1918, Marshall Foch called for an Allied offensive all along the line. The British had control of the northern sector, which cut through Belgium, and the offensive pointed like a knife at the heart of Germany. The French controlled the southern sector, which lay along the Rhine, all the way to the border with Switzerland. The Americans were in between their two allies.

The Allied offensive began in July. The Americans did very well in the area around Amiens, an old cathedral city in the heart of France. Pershing's men cut through the German lines, taking more prisoners than anyone anticipated. With each passing day, the German high command came to respect, and perhaps fear, the Americans more. On one occasion, Field Marshall von Hindenburg burst into exasperated tones. He could not believe, he shouted, that two German divisions could not contain one American.

Of course, there were times when progress was not rapid. The hot, dry days of July and August proved the best for the Allied fighters. When the rains came in September, they slowed down the Allied offensives. But the Americans still had surprises up their sleeves. One of the most stunning of these came on October 8, 1918.

# Sergeant York

Born in rural Tennessee in 1887, Alvin York shared some things in common with Woodrow Wilson. Like the president, York came from rural people of deep piety. Like the president, Alvin York was a person of deep, though quiet, religious feeling. Like Woodrow Wilson, York was a Southerner, someone who believed in the values and virtues of the South. Unlike the president, however, Alvin York was a first-rate sharpshooter.

Growing up, York hunted chipmunks and rabbits. When he was drafted in 1917, York declared himself a conscientious objector. He changed his mind, however, and soon rose to corporal in the US. Army. In October 1918, York and his regiment were in a wooded area in northeastern France, rather close to the German border. York and a small patrol got behind German lines, where, to their astonishment, they found the Germans on the verge of giving up. Separated from his patrol, Sergeant York killed roughly twenty-three Germans with his rifle, and brought 130 others back as prisoners. His was the single most outstanding result achieved by any American in the war.

York became a hero and a sensation. His valor showed the skill of the average US soldier, and his exploit was yet another indication that the war was coming to an end.

# The Meuse-Argonne Offensive

By October 1918, the Allied forces were winning on all fronts. Marshal Ferdinand Foch, naturally, wanted the greatest glory for his French soldiers, but General Pershing's Americans were well placed to deliver the final knockout

Tennessean Alvin C. York meant to be a conscientious objector, but he became America's number-one war hero.

blow. Pershing drew up the plans, but their execution depended on Captain George C. Marshall, who later became an outstanding American chief of staff in the Second World War.

More than a million men and thousands of pieces of artillery had to be moved from one sector of the front to another. An incredible number of Springfield rifles had to be issued, and the Americans also used a few tanks in this last phase of the war. By the first of November, the Americans had pierced the Siegfried Line, Germany's number-one line of defense.

Watching from Washington, DC, President Wilson was elated. Not only were the Americans performing minor miracles on the ground, but they also did so in ways that reflected with high credit on the nation. Wilson was aware that he stood in an unusual, nearly a unique, position. No previous American president except Abraham Lincoln had ever placed so many men in the field, and Lincoln had not lived long enough to enjoy the fruits of victory.

Each passing day brought more peace feelers from the Central Powers. Wilson would like to have given them more consideration, but events on the ground moved too rapidly. Bulgaria, the Ottoman Empire, and Austria-Hungary all gave up the fight by the first of November. Imperial Germany stood alone.

# Abdication

Kaiser Wilhelm II was only a shadow of the man who had looked so strong when the war began. His nerves shot, his confidence broken, the kaiser mistakenly believed that the German military was still loyal to him. Early in November

## From Captains and Colonels to Generals and Admirals

Many American officers were young men in World War I, and middle-aged men in World War II. Many benefited from their World War I training, which readied them for World War II. The short list includes George S. Patton, Dwight D. Eisenhower, George C. Marshall, and Douglas MacArthur. On the naval side, Chester Nimitz and Ernest J. King are good examples of men who rose from captain and lieutenant in World War I to admiral in World War II.

1918, the kaiser even contemplated turning the army on the civilian population, to force the loyalty of the common folk. At this point, his leading generals informed him that the army was still loyal to Germany, but that it no longer followed his lead. Accepting this bitter pill, the kaiser abdicated his throne and fled into exile in Holland.

## Surrender

On November 8, 1918, with the kaiser still (just barely) in Germany, German leaders put out desperate peace feelers. President Wilson wished he was on the scene, to act as the arbiter, but the power was in the hands of the French military commanders. They required their German counterparts to meet them in a railroad car at Compiègne, on the morning of November 11, 1918.

General Pershing with Colonel George C. Marshall, who became famous for his service in World War II.

The German generals made one last forlorn effort, asking what kind of terms Marshall Foch would offer. The marshal turned a stony face to them, saying he had no terms to offer. Either Germany accepted the armistice, or the war would go on. The Germans signed the document, and the word went out, all up and down the long lines, that the fighting should come to a stop.

The Great War was over. Perhaps fifteen million lives had been lost. Enormous sections of ground, in northern France and in Belgium, as well as in Poland and western Russia, had been torn up by various invading armies. The world was not the same as it had been in 1914.

# Rejoicing

Americans got the news on November 11, 1918. They turned out in all the major cities for celebrations the likes of which had never before been seen. The end of the Civil War in 1865 had been greeted in hushed tones and understatement. The end of the Great War in 1918 was accompanied by parades, marching bands, and what seemed like boundless enthusiasm.

President Wilson and the First lady were not above the popular enthusiasm. They were as affected as anyone else. The First Couple could scarcely believe their good luck. The nation had made enormous efforts, and there had been dissent, but the results spoke for themselves. In November 1918, the United States was one of the few nations in the world that had more than enough food for its people to eat. America had also become the world's largest creditor nation. Most of the Allied nations owed large sums to American industrial and manufacturing concerns.

The railroad car in which the Armistice was signed on
November 11, 1918.

# The Spanish Flu

Wilson had indeed led the nation in war. He was about to lead it in peace. One thing Wilson had no answer for was the Spanish flu, short for influenza. In the autumn of 1918, many returning American soldiers came home sick, and the naval bases on the East Coast soon became breeding grounds for the disease. More Americans lost their lives from the flu than from German bullets or bombs in the Great War.

America had not won the war all on its own. A great effort by many nations was necessary. But without America, the war either would have been lost or would have ended in a deadly standoff. Only America in 1918 had both the muscle power on the ground and the financial capital to finance the war.

## Wilson's Plan

The precise moment at which President Wilson made his decision is not known. Toward the end of November 1918, he announced his intention to leave Washington, DC, and travel to Europe, where he could lead America at the peace table.

To Wilson and the First Lady, this decision made abundant sense. The prime minister of Britain and the premier of France, as well as the prime minister of Italy would all be at the peace settlement. It made sense for the American

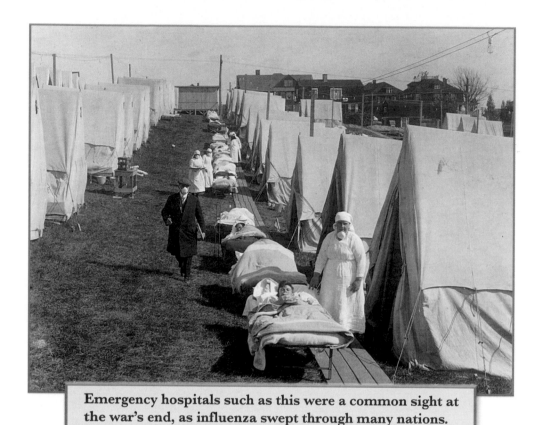

**Emergency hospitals such as this were a common sight at the war's end, as influenza swept through many nations.**

president to be there, too. Wilson's decision overlooked something very significant, however. No other American president had ever left the country for any substantial period of time.

George Washington never left America, save for a short trip to Barbados in his youth. James Madison was in Washington, DC, throughout the War of 1812, except for the brief period of time when the British captured the city. And Abraham Lincoln never set foot out of the United States. Four long years of civil war found him constantly in the White House.

There was—and is—no law or constitutional require-
ment that the president remain in Washington, DC. But
President Wilson took a big chance when he decided
to leave the capital city. He could not be certain that the
mood of jubilation would last, or that the leaders of the
US Congress would agree with everything he did overseas.

# THE BIG FOUR

**O**n December 4, 1918, President Wilson and First Lady
Edith Bolling Galt Wilson went aboard the *George Washington*,
headed for France. They came ashore in Brittany ten days
later, and were celebrated and made the toast of the town.
Nothing, not even America's success in the war, prepared
Wilson for the adulation he received from the crowds.

The French could not get enough of Wilson. From low
to high, they seemed to think Wilson would bring about
a new and more peaceful world. When the First Couple
departed for England, they encountered more of the same.
And when the Wilsons traveled by train to Rome, they
experienced even more adulation.

Wilson thoroughly enjoyed the crowds. He had long
been an instinctive politician, a person who senses the
mood of a crowd. As he departed Italy, however, Wilson
expressed sadness. He would not fight for Italy to get the
land its people wanted so badly, he declared to his wife.
And the crowds that cheered him at this point might well
turn against him.

96

Wilson on his way to France, in December 1918.

## The Versailles Peace Conference

When the Wilsons returned to Paris, they found the leaders and delegations of most of the nations present in the City of Light. Great Britain was represented by Prime Minister Lloyd George. France put forward Premier Georges Clemenceau. And Italy sent Prime Minister Vittorio Orlando. These men were referred to as the "Big Four," meaning that they held great power.

Many other nations were represented at Versailles. Of the major powers, only two were not consulted. Germany was regarded as the villain, the nation that started the war. Germany was not allowed any representatives at the peace talks. Russia was regarded as having passed out of the bounds of civilization.

Early in the discussions, it was asked who would preside over the deliberations. President Wilson proposed Premier Clemenceau, who was happy to take that position. At that

## The Tiger

Georges Clemenceau, nicknamed the "Tiger," was seventy-three when the Big Four met at Versailles. He was old, but Clemenceau had an excellent memory. Like Woodrow Wilson, he remembered the American Civil War. Clemenceau had been in America during the war. He had even married an American. But if one thinks this would make him more sympathetic to Wilson, or the American approach to peace, he or she was very much mistaken.

The Big Four—Wilson, George, Orlando, and Clemenceau—
at one of their early meetings.

moment, the president underestimated the premier's sentiments. Wilson did not realize how deep was Clemenceau's
desire for revenge on Germany.

# The Question of Germany

The Big Four, and the delegations of many nations, faced
many questions. The single biggest one, however, had to do
with Germany.

France felt a strong need to punish Germany. The
people of Belgium felt much the same. The British were
split roughly down the middle. Quite a few wanted to
punish Germany. They even carried signs that said "Hang

the Kaiser." Britain had not suffered as much as France, however, and many English men and women believed it would be better to let Germany off rather lightly.

Of all the Allied leaders, President Wilson was the one friendliest to Germany. He despised Kaiser Wilhelm II, and the imperial regime he once led, but once the German Empire shifted to the German republic, Wilson showed a good deal of sympathy. He wanted to see Germany reduced in terms of military strength, but for her economic strength to remain in place.

## The Question of Austria-Hungary

Americans, English, and French had one thing in common— they all were inclined to let Austria-Hungary off the hook. World War I commenced shortly after the assassination of the Austrian archduke, but the Austrians had never faced Americans on the battlefield. The typical American, therefore, was not angry with Austria.

Then, too, the old Austro-Hungarian Empire lay in ruins. For three centuries, the Austrian Habsburgs presided over a multiethnic empire that spanned Eastern Europe and the Balkan Mountains. Now the entire area was politically a no-man's-land, with no one in control. And, as bad as things were in what had previously been Czarist Russia.

## The Special Case of Russia

What had previously been Czarist Russia, or the Russian Empire, no longer existed. Instead, there was a brand-new Bolshevik government in Moscow and in St. Petersburg, and great confusion in the countryside. It was by no means

| | Sq Miles | Population |
|---|---|---|
| FINLAND | 125,000 | 3,250,000 |
| BALTIC PRS (ESTHONIA, LIVONIA & COURLAND) | 35,000 | 5,000,000 |
| POLAND | 45,000 | 12,250,000 |
| LITHUANIA | 80,000 | 8,500,000 |
| UKRAINE | 150,000 | 28,000,000 |
| Total | 435,000 | 55,000,000 |

Germany grabbed several Eastern European nations at the Treaty of Brest-Litovsk. Wilson intended for those nations, and peoples, to enjoy national self-determination.

certain whether Lenin and Trotsky would consolidate their power and establish a true Communist regime.

For all of the Big Four—Wilson, Orlando, Lloyd George, and Clemenceau—Russia was the great unknown. For all four nations—America, Italy, Britain, and France—Russia was an enormous question mark. Would it ever return to become part of the capitalist world?

# Italy and Japan

Italy and Japan were both part of the Allied war effort, but neither nation had covered itself in glory. Japan had snapped up dozens of German-held islands in the Pacific, but that was the extent of its energy. Italy had fought against Austria-Hungary for three long years. Italy had taken many casualties, and its people wanted land, but neither Wilson nor Lloyd George believed they had earned it. If the Big Four granted a wide swathe of territory to Italy, this might upset the chances for effecting a lasting settlement in the Balkans.

To say that the Big Four confronted great obstacles is an understatement.

# Wilson Heads Home

In February 1919, President Wilson and his wife went home aboard the *George Washington*. Wilson felt the need to see what was happening at home. Greeted by a tumultuous welcome in Boston, the president headed to Washington, DC, where he was received with scant praise. The elections of 1918 had returned Republican majorities in both Houses of Congress. Wilson would no longer have his way.

Throughout his presidency, Wilson had been able to move Congress, to persuade its leaders to see things his way. There was no guarantee that this would continue, however.

Disappointed by the congressional response, Wilson soon returned to France (again aboard the *George Washington*). There, too, he experienced a lessening in what had been such strong public sentiment. Less than three months had passed since his first arrival, but the Parisians no longer shouted and waved as before. Perhaps they sensed Wilson would not be able to deliver on all he had promised.

Typically, Wilson vowed to double his efforts.

# The Final Negotiations

The Big Four held immense power, but they could not get along with each other. By mid-spring of 1919, it was evident that Wilson was on one side, and Lloyd George and Clemenceau on the other. Vittorio Orlando continued to participate in the meetings of the Big Four, but he had less influence than before.

Could Wilson have gained all that he wanted? The answer is negative. Wilson had set forth such an ambitious agenda through the Fourteen Points that it was impossible for him to attain all his goals. The president believed, however, that all would be well, as long as the League of Nations was established. Toward that end, he directed all his energies.

In July 1919, the German diplomats were brought to the Palace at Versailles and shown the peace treaty. When they spoke of negotiation, they were told, quite firmly, that negotiation was out of the question. Either they signed the document, or the Allies would start the war over once more. Bending their heads, the German representatives signed.

The Treaty of Versailles clearly stated that Imperial Germany bore the guilt of causing the First World War. Germany, now a republic, was stripped of 13 percent of its territory, and forbidden to have any navy or an army of more than one hundred thousand men. In addition, a large reparations figure—which had yet to be determined—would be levied on Germany.

The Austro-Hungarian Empire no longer existed. In its place, six new nations were established. A much smaller Austria emerged, followed by Czechoslovakia, Hungary, and other nations. And in the north, a new Poland was established. The twelfth of Wilson's Fourteen Points proved the strongest.

Italy gained some land along the Adriatic Sea, but it was small compared to what the Italians wanted. Japan gained title to the Pacific Islands it possessed during the war. And even when all these decisions were made, one item simply went unaccounted for. No one knew what to say, much less what to do, about Bolshevik Russia.

## Wilson and the League

Wilson walked out of the peace negotiations with his head held high. He looked as firm and in control as ever. But this was just a perception, one which he labored to create. In truth, Wilson was physically exhausted, as well as deeply disappointed. He had been outmaneuvered by Clemenceau and Lloyd George. The Peace of Versailles was punitive in the extreme.

This photograph shows the first meeting of the League of Nations.

Wilson continued to cling to one hope and belief. As long as the League of Nations got off the ground, all could be made well in the end. A genuine international body was required, to ensure tragedies such as the First World War never happened again. And there, in Article 31 of the treaty, were the words that gave birth to the League.

Wilson sailed for home. The *George Washington*, again, served as his means of transport. On the return voyage, Wilson and his wife enjoyed the company of Franklin D. Roosevelt and his wife, Eleanor. Wilson saw something charming and vital in the young man, but he did not anticipate that Roosevelt would one day live in the White House, or that he would one day confront evils and dangers even more severe than those posed by the First World War.

# WILSON'S LEGACY

**R**eturning home, President Wilson found the situation much altered. He had been away for the better part of seven months. In that time, the Republican leaders in the US Senate and House had done much of the day-to-day governing of the nation.

Wilson came home with one major objective. He wanted the Senate to confirm the Versailles Treaty, and for America to participate in the League of Nations. Given all that America had accomplished during the war, and all of Wilson's labors in France, it seemed quite likely that this would happen.

Wilson miscalculated, however.

## Senator Lodge

For the better part of a decade, Senator Henry Cabot Lodge, of Massachusetts, had been President Wilson's strongest opponent. The differences between them had a political basis, but they went well beyond it. In fact, the two men held each other in disdain.

Henry Cabot Lodge was Wilson's deadly political foe. Lodge helped kill American participation in the League of Nations.

Wilson regarded Senator Lodge as an obstructionist. He saw Lodge as someone who wished to spoil something—the League of Nations—rather than someone who wanted to create something new. For his part, Senator Lodge regarded the president as a hopeless idealist, someone who could not see the facts as they were.

Lodge and Wilson prepared for the final struggle. Each man knew that the other would give it his all.

## Headed West

In September 1919, Wilson decided that only one good option remained. Throughout his career, Wilson had done better with the average voter than with the established politicians. He, therefore, decided to appeal to the conscience of the common American. The best, perhaps only, way to do this was to make a railroad trip.

Newspapers did not carry the sound of a person's voice. Radio was in its infancy. The only way Wilson knew was to make a trip and speak directly to the voters. It made sense, too, to address his speeches primarily to voters in the western states. The West had handed Wilson his reelection victory in 1916.

On September 3, 1919, Wilson, his wife, and a large group of aides boarded the *Mayflower*, the presidential railroad car, and headed out of Washington. The first major stop was in Columbus, Ohio, where Wilson gave a lengthy speech at Memorial Hall. Right from the outset, it was clear that the president retained a special bond with common Americans. The people of Columbus cheered him lustily.

Wilson spoke in Richmond, Indiana, in Indianapolis, and then in St. Louis. Once he departed Illinois, Wilson

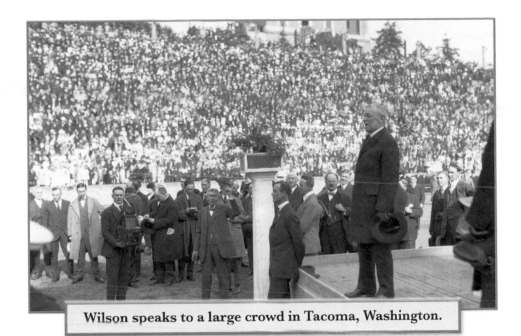

**Wilson speaks to a large crowd in Tacoma, Washington.**

was in the West, and the tempo of his speeches increased. He spoke in Des Moines, Iowa; Omaha, Nebraska; and Sioux Falls, South Dakota. He traveled to Minneapolis and St. Paul, Minnesota, and then headed to California. Almost everywhere he spoke, Wilson struck a sympathetic chord, but he enjoyed his greatest success in Los Angeles, where two hundred thousand people turned out to see and hear him. From there it was on to Salt Lake City, and then Pueblo, Colorado. And that was where disaster struck.

Wilson's physician, Dr. Cary T. Grayson, had watched with concern and anxiety throughout the railroad trip. The president made magnificent speeches, but he was then left completely exhausted. Matters became worse with each major stop, and in Pueblo, Wilson was so ill he could barely see. All through the trip he had experienced headaches, but these now became incapacitating.

Wilson managed to complete his speech in Pueblo, but he was in terrible shape that evening. Wilson confided in Dr. Grayson, saying "I seem to have gone to pieces … I am not in condition to go on."[1]

The presidential train headed back to Washington, DC.

## Invalid in the White House

Days after returning to Washington, Wilson suffered a major stroke. Those who study his medical record believe he may have suffered several small ones over the previous two decades. This stroke, however, robbed him of feeling on one side of his body (the left) and confined him to his bed in the White House. Wilson's mind seemed unimpaired, but his physical incapacity was beyond doubt.

While Wilson lived the life of an invalid, the US Senate debated the Versailles Treaty. Beyond any doubt, Wilson's

## The First Lady

Edith Bolling Galt Wilson was completely devoted to her husband. She wished him to recover his health. Toward that end, she helped conceal his true condition. The Cabinet did not meet for several months. During that time, the First Lady and Dr. Grayson were the only people to have regular, unfettered access to the president. Historians have accused Mrs. Wilson of acting as a surrogate president. In truth, she was a frightened person, who cared about her husband first, and the national interest second.

## Treaties and the Senate

The US Constitution is quite clear about the making of treaties. The president, as commander in chief, has the right to negotiate treaties. Only the Senate can approve them, however, and the vote must be at least two-thirds in favor. Fifty-three Senators voted to accept the Versailles Treaty. Only thirty-eight negative votes were registered, but these were sufficient to deny Wilson the necessary two-thirds majority.

physical weakness made his political situation worse. The president was unable to appear before Congress, and to employ the speech making which had long been his great strength. It has to be admitted, however, that Wilson took a bad situation and made it even worse.

When the Senate developed a list of changes that the Republican majority wanted, Wilson refused them on virtually every count. He would not brook any changes in the Versailles Treaty, he said, because he needed to honor the sacrifice made by so many young Americans in the war. On one occasion, the First Lady implored Wilson to make some compromise with the Senate Republicans. His answer, delivered from his bed, was emphatic.

"Can't you see," Wilson said, "that I have no moral right to accept any chance in a paper I have signed without giving to every other signatory, even the Germans, the right to do the same thing? It is not I that will not accept it; it is the Nation's honor that is at stake."[2]

In moral terms, the president was at least half right. In political terms, his decision, and stance, amounted to the end of his career.

The US Senate rejected the Versailles Treaty on March 19, 1920, by a vote of 53–38.

## End of the War

America never fully "left" the First World War. The Versailles Treaty was not approved, and there was no official

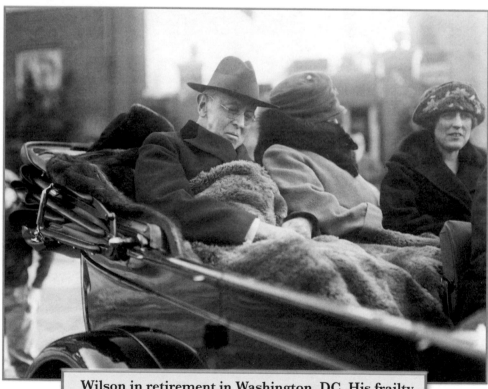

**Wilson in retirement in Washington, DC. His frailty was apparent to all who saw him.**

end to the Great War. The results of the war were plain to see, however.

The United States came out of World War I in a much stronger condition than it had ever previously known. In 1919 and 1920, Wall Street bankers possessed a greater share of the world's wealth than those of London and Paris combined. America, too, was the only nation that had nothing to fear from its neighbors.

The American doughboy had shown his mettle. American sailors, soldiers, and Marines had achieved great things during the Great War. No one would ever take American military power lightly again.

At the same time, America had suffered real losses. Not only had 52,000 men died in battle, but another 60,000 died either from battle wounds or as the result of disease. And the great crusade, the war to make the world safe for democracy, left a sour taste in the mouths of many Americans. Throughout the 1920s, and well into the 1930s, a majority of Americans expressed their distaste for any more "foreign wars."

The United States came out of the First World War with an enhanced profile in the wider world. Americans, however, were not keen to take on any new responsibilities. The watchword for the next two decades was "isolationism."

And what of the man who had led the nation to victory?

# Wilson's Last Years

Tragic is the only word that can encompass the final years of Wilson's life. The man of abundant physical, moral, and intellectual energy was reduced to an invalid, living quietly in Washington, DC.

On March 4, 1921, Wilson joined Republican Warren G. Harding for a short automobile ride from the White House to the Capitol building. Harding had been elected in a landslide four months earlier, and his election was a clear repudiation of Wilson's policies. Many Americans retained affection for the president, but they chose Harding and the Republicans.

Retiring from public life, Mr. and Mrs. Wilson lived a quiet life on S Street, close to Dupont Circle in the nation's capital. On rare occasions, Wilson gave short speeches to the press, but for the most part he was on the sidelines. Wilson died in Washington in February 1924. He was sixty-seven years old.

# From the First to the Second World War

From his sickbed, Wilson prophesied, with frightening accuracy, the coming of the Second World War. The punitive peace treaty inflicted on Germany was the greatest mistake, Wilson declared, but American refusal to join the League of Nations was the second.

For a decade after Wilson's death, it seemed that the president's prediction would not come true. Virtually all of the nations of the Western world experienced some prosperity in the late 1920s; nearly all of them were subsequently plunged into the Great Depression in the 1930s. It seemed that the leaders and nations of the world had more important matters than war to consider. But in January 1933, the same month that Franklin D. Roosevelt was inaugurated president of the United States, Adolf Hitler was sworn in as chancellor of Germany.

The road to the Second World War began in the throes of the Great Depression.

## Stronger the Second Time Around

Though Wilson has been criticized for many things, one can argue that he left America much stronger than he found it. The size of the Regular US Army doubled during his time in the White House, and America's capacity for making war substantially increased. Many of the ideas, plans, and programs Wilson put into practice in 1917–1918 came to their full fruition a generation later, in 1941–1945. Of course, it is ironic that a man who loved peace, and who valued moral development and logic over military might, presided over one of the great leaps forward of the United States as a military power.

# CONCLUSION

When Woodrow Wilson died in 1924, the world was quite different from the one that existed a decade earlier, just prior to the outbreak of war. Not only had millions of men clashed on the battlefield and left their bones in foreign lands. The world was also altered by the onrush of new technologies.

The machine gun, hand grenade, submarine, and military airplane had all demonstrated deadly efficacy in the Great War. The tank had not appeared in time to make a major impact, but there was little doubt it would be very important in the future. Beyond these military technologies, however, was a major difference in how the common person looked, acted, and felt.

Americans wanted to forget all about the Great War. Warren G. Harding won the White House in 1920 with his pledge of a return to "normalcy." In truth, however, neither Americans nor their contemporaries could turn back the clock. Something very significant had changed.

A deep pessimism gripped Americans where the rest of the world was concerned. During the 1920s, Americans delighted in the use of all sorts of new gadgets, including the automobile, the radio, and even commonplace articles such as the refrigerator. Music and dance, too, burst forth as never before, as jazz became America's number-one contribution to the art of that time. Just beneath the release of pent-up enthusiasm was a deep cynicism, however.

Americans were certain they did not wish to be involved in foreign wars. Though they had accomplished great things on the battlefield, they felt they had lost the peace. This was not strictly true, but it was how Americans felt. Therefore, when the roar of the Twenties turned into the Great Depression of the Thirties, Americans vowed to stay out of any foreign entanglements. Perhaps they should have listened to the prophetic words of Woodrow Wilson.

When he was in Paris, negotiating the Versailles Treaty, Wilson declared that this peace must be just, or else the world would experience another terrible war. When he lay prostrate, in the White House, crippled by his stroke, the president declared that the senators who blocked passage of the treaty were asking for another world war.

The final words of statesmen are not always prophetic. Many great leaders descend in the last years of their lives and become mere shadows of their former selves. Where the First World War is concerned, the prophecies of two great statesmen stand out. The first is Otto von Bismarck. Known as Germany's "Iron Chancellor," Bismarck was the effective ruler of that nation between 1871 and 1888. During those years, he declared, time and again, that if the world went to war again, it would be because of some unexpected incident in the Balkans.

Bismarck turned out to be right. The assassination of Franz Ferdinand in June 1914 was the match that lit the powder keg of the First World War. Woodrow Wilson also was right. The harsh, punitive treaty that ended the First World War made the Second World War likely.

# CHRONOLOGY

**1856**

Woodrow Wilson is born in Staunton, Virginia.

**1859**

The Wilson family moves to Georgia.

**1865**

The Civil War ends in Confederate defeat.

**1871**

The Franco-Prussian War ends in German victory and the establishment of the German Empire.

**1879**

Wilson graduates from Princeton University.

**1902**

Wilson becomes president of Princeton University.

**1910**

Wilson runs for and is elected governor of New Jersey.

**1912**

Wilson wins a three-way race for the White House.

**1913**

Wilson and his family move into the White House. The first Wilson administration begins.

**1914**

Archduke Franz Ferdinand is assassinated on June 28.
Austria declares war on Serbia on July 28.
Britain declares was on Imperial Germany on August 4.

Ellen Axson Wilson dies at the White House on August 6.

Wilson issues a declaration of American neutrality on
August 19.

## 1915

The *Lusitania* sunk by German submarine on May 7.

Wilson marries Edith Bolling Galt on December 17.

## 1916

Charles Evans Hughes wins the Republican
presidential nomination.

Wilson wins reelection on November 7.

## 1917

Imperial Germany announces unrestricted submarine
warfare on January 31.

Wilson breaks diplomatic relations with Germany on
February 7.

British intelligence intercepts the Zimmermann Telegram.

Wilson asks Congress for declaration of war on April 2.

Wilson signs the declaration on April 6.

The Creel Committee is formed on April 13.

Drawings of Selective service numbers begins in June.

Wilson seizes the railroads, and appropriates them for
wartime use.

## 1918

Wilson delivers the Fourteen Points speech to Congress on
January 8.

US forces win the Battle of Belleau Wood in France
in June.

American forces lead the way in the Meuse-Argonne Offensive.

Sergeant Alvin C. York carries out the single-most successful action in the war.

The First World War ends on November 11.

Wilson sails for France aboard the *George Washington* on December 4.

## 1919

Wilson returns from France, arriving in Boston on February 23.

Wilson sails for France again, this time from New Jersey, on March 5.

Wilson returns to America in August.

Wilson embarks on a railroad speaking tour in September.

Wilson collapses while giving a speech in Pueblo, Colorado, on September 25.

## 1920

The Senate rejects the Treaty of Versailles.

Warren G. Harding and Calvin Coolidge win the White House.

Wilson and the First Lady leave the White House on March 4.

## 1924

Wilson dies in Washington, DC, on February 4.

# CHAPTER NOTES

## CHAPTER 1 WILSON BEFORE THE CONGRESS

1. "Wilson's War Message to Congress," online at www.lib.byu.edu.
2. *Selected Literary and Political Papers and Addresses of Woodrow Wilson*, 3 vols. (New York, NY: Grosset & Dunlap, 1926, vol. 2): 236.
3. Ibid, p. 238.
4. Ibid, p. 241.
5. Ibid, p. 241.
6. Ibid, p. 244.
7. Ibid, p. 247.
8. Ibid.
9. Ibid.
10. *New York Times* (April 6, 1917):

## CHAPTER 3 THE FIRST WORLD WAR BEGINS

1. *New York Times* (June 29 1914): 1.
2. Mario R. DiNunzio, ed., *Woodrow Wilson: Essential Writings and Speeches of the Scholar-President* (New York, NY: New York University Press, 2006), p. 390.
3. Ibid, p. 391.
4. "The American Presidency Project," online at http://www.presidency.ucsb.edu/.

## CHAPTER 5 ADMIRALS AND GENERALS

1. John Perry, *Pershing: Commander of the Great War* (Nashville, TN: Thomas Nelson, 2011).
2. Ibid.
3. Ibid.

## CHAPTER 6  THE WAR AT HOME

1. *Selected Literary and Political Papers and Addresses of Woodrow Wilson*, 3 vols. (New York, NY: Grosset & Dunlap, 1926, vol. 2), p. 251.
2. Ibid.
3. Mario R. DiNunzio, ed., *Woodrow Wilson: Essential Writings and Speeches of the Scholar-President* (New York, NY: New York University Press, 2006), p. 404.
4. Ibid.
5. Ibid.
6. Ibid.
7. Ibid, p. 406.
8. Ibid.

## CHAPTER 10  WILSON'S LEGACY

1. Scott Berg, *Wilson* (New York, NY: Berkley Books, 2013), p. 636.
2. Ibid, p. 655

# GLOSSARY

**armaments**  The arms, weapons, and gunpowder that exist within a nation's arsenal

**armistice**  A temporary end to hostilities

**capital**  The capital city of a country or nation

**capitol**  The actual building that houses the nerve center of a government

**convoy**  A group of ships, buses, or trucks carrying material

**covenant**  A sacred agreement

**dissent**  To dissent is to disagree. In wartime, dissent is often frowned upon.

**entourage**  The people around a leading person, as in the security personnel surrounding a chief executive

**influenza**  A serious form of respiratory illness, which can be fatal if not treated

**materiel**  This refers to war materials, such as gunpowder, rifles, etc.

**national self-determination**  The right of a people to determine their shape and form of national government

**neurotic**  A neurotic individual is pushed one way and then the other by his or her internal conflicts

**peace table**  The place where diplomats arrange a permanent end to hostilities

**piety**  To show piety is to demonstrate religious devotion

**plurality**  To win the largest number of votes, while not obtaining an outright majority

**podium**  The central place, or spot, from which speeches are made

**regalia**  A special costume, usually to show an individual's status, as in the robes of a judge

**Regular Army**  The United States Regular Army was separate from the various militia units which could be mobilized in short order

# FURTHER READING

## BOOKS

Aronin, Miriam. *World War I*, online resource. Bearport Publishing, 2016.

Lanser, Amanda. *World War I through the Eyes of Woodrow Wilson*, online resource. Core Library, 2016.

Stone, Tanya Lee. *The Progressive Era and World War I*. New York, NY: Steck-Vaughn, 2001.

Uschan, Michael V. *The 1910s: A Cultural History of the United States Through The Decades*. San Diego, CA: Lucent Books, 1999.

## WEBSITES

**John J. Pershing Papers—Library of Congress**
https://www.loc.gov/collections/john-pershing-papers/

**Papers of Woodrow Wilson—The American Presidency Project**
www.presidency.ucsb.edu/woodrow_wilson.php

**Treaty of Versailles**
https://www.britannica.com/event/Treaty-of-Versailles-1919

**World War I and America**
http://wwiamerica.org/

# INDEX

## A

American Expeditionary
    Force, 55
Axson, Ellen Lousie, 21-22,
    30, 36

## B

Baker, Newton, 49, 50, 55,
    57, 66
Black Hand, 32

## C

Carnegie, Andrew, 24
Clemenceau, George, 98,
    99, 102, 103, 104
Committee on Public
    Information, 49, 67, 68
Creel, George, 49, 67, 68
Czar Nicholas II, 32, 43

## D

Daniels, Josephus, 49, 50
draft of 1918, 47, 66

## E

election of 1912, 27-28
election of 1916, 39, 41
election of 1920, 116

## F

Ferdinand, Franz, 31, 82,
    86, 118
Five Minute Men, 68

Foch, Marshal Ferdinand,
    82, 83, 85, 86, 91
Fourteen Points, 70-73, 103,
    104

## G

Galt, Edith Bolling, 38, 39,
    96, 110
George, Lloyd, 98, 102,
    103, 104

## H

Haig, Sir Douglas, 57
Harding, Warren G., 114,
    116
Hughes, Charles Evans, 41

## I

Imperial Germany,
    crisis with, 9, 11-12
    defeat of, 84-85, 89, 91
    in World War I, 42, 45,
        75-77

## J

Jellicoe, Sir John, 51, 53
Johns Hopkins University,
    21, 49

## K

Kaiser Wilhelm II
    abdication, 88-89
    leadership, 11, 32, 75,
Keller, Helen, 67